Robert Armin

Fools and Jesters

Elibron Classics
www.elibron.com

Elibron Classics series.

© 2007 Adamant Media Corporation.

ISBN 1-4021-4622-1 (paperback)
ISBN 1-4212-7585-6 (hardcover)

This Elibron Classics Replica Edition is an unabridged facsimile
of the edition published in 1842 by the Shakespeare Society, London.

Elibron and Elibron Classics are trademarks of
Adamant Media Corporation. All rights reserved.

This book is an accurate reproduction of the original. Any marks, names, colophons, imprints, logos or other symbols or identifiers that appear on or in this book, except for those of Adamant Media Corporation and BookSurge, LLC, are used only for historical reference and accuracy and are not meant to designate origin or imply any sponsorship by or license from any third party.

FOOLS AND JESTERS;

WITH A

REPRINT OF ROBERT ARMIN'S

NEST OF NINNIES.

1608.

WITH AN INTRODUCTION AND NOTES.

LONDON:
PRINTED FOR THE SHAKESPEARE SOCIETY.

1842.

LONDON :
P. SHOBERL, JUN., 51, RUPERT STREET, HAYMARKET,
PRINTER TO H. R. H. PRINCE ALBERT.

COUNCIL
OF
THE SHAKESPEARE SOCIETY.

President.

THE MOST NOBLE THE MARQUESS OF NORMANBY.

Vice-Presidents.

RT. HON. LORD BRAYBROOKE, F.S.A.
RT. HON. LORD F. EGERTON, M.P.
RT. HON. THE EARL OF GLENGALL.
RT. HON. EARL HOWE.
RT. HON. LORD LEIGH.
RT. HON. THE EARL OF POWIS.

AMYOT, THOMAS, ESQ., F.R.S., TREAS. S. A.
AYRTON, WILLIAM, ESQ., F.R.S., F.S.A.
BOTFIELD, BERIAH, ESQ., M.P.
BRUCE, JOHN, ESQ., F.S.A.
COLLIER, J. PAYNE, ESQ., F.S.A., DIRECTOR.
CRAIK, GEORGE L., ESQ.
CUNNINGHAM, PETER, ESQ., TREASURER.
DYCE, REV. ALEXANDER.
FIELD, BARRON, ESQ.
HALLAM, HENRY, ESQ., F.R.S., V.P.S.A.
HALLIWELL, J. O., ESQ., F.R.S. F.S.A.
HARNESS, REV. WILLIAM.
MACREADY, WILLIAM C., ESQ.
MILMAN, REV. HENRY HART.
OXENFORD, JOHN, ESQ.
PETTIGREW, T. J., ESQ., F.R.S., F.S.A.
PLANCHÉ, J. R., ESQ., F.S.A.
THOMS, WILLIAM J., ESQ., F.S.A.
TOMLINS, F. GUEST, ESQ., SECRETARY.
WATSON, SIR FREDERICK BEILBY, K.C.H., F.R.S.
WRIGHT, THOMAS, ESQ., M.A., F.S.A.

INTRODUCTION.

It would be singular that a man of so much, and of such peculiar, learning as the late Mr. Douce, in his "Dissertation upon Clowns and Fools," should not even refer to the ensuing tract, did we not know that only a single copy of it (as far as has been ascertained by the most diligent inquiries during the last thirty or forty years) exists in any public or private collection. Were it, therefore, of less value than it really possesses, as a curious picture of manners, towards the end of the reign of Elizabeth, and in the beginning of that of James I., we should be disposed to reprint it, in order to place it beyond the possibility of destruction. The original is preserved in the Bodleian Library, the statutes of which, we believe, forbid fire within the precincts of the edifice; and the unceasing and almost affectionate care of the Rev. Dr. Bandinel and his curators inspires every confidence as to the security of the matchless stores in their custody: still we are unwilling that any volume of this description, of which no other exemplar is known, should be exposed to the slightest risk of loss, however remote or improbable. We mention this as an additional inducement with us for the republication of a relic of much interest and merit, not only *unique* in itself, but unprecedented in its kind. The tract is the only one in our language that treats distinctly of such a subject, and of such persons, as the domestic fools and jesters of a period when they began to receive less encouragement than they had experienced in times of greater ignorance and barbarism.

The entertainment of this class of persons in private families seems to have originated mainly in two causes: one of these was, that the care and custody of idiots was of old assigned to individuals as a source of emolument, the latter having the control and management of the estates of the former: another cause was, perhaps, the natural weakness of our nature, which, when any species of learning was a rare acquisition, and when intellectual abilities were less prized and cultivated, sought to place itself in contrast with those who would show off to advantage even the smallest acquirements, and the most moderate talents. This consideration will account for the ancient familiarity of great men, even of kings and princes, with their fools or jesters, and for the introduction of them at their tables, on the most solemn, as well as on the most festive occasions. It has been ascertained, and requires no proof here, that such was the case of old, not merely in England, but in most other countries of Europe.

It is not our intention at present to pursue this inquiry farther, but merely to observe that the fools, to whose propensities and adventures the following pages chiefly relate, belonged to the class usually entertained in the houses of the nobility and gentry. There can be no doubt that the dramatic clowns and fools, such as they are represented in the plays of Shakespeare and his contemporaries, originated in this practice; although they came down to the poets of the end of the sixteenth and of the beginning of the seventeenth century, through the medium of the personage who is known as the Vice of the old Moralities: he was employed in them, sometimes by his affected stolidity, and at others by his low cunning, to amuse the spectators, and to relieve their minds from the weight of the more serious portions of the performance. In this point of view, all that relates to the history of the domestic fool cannot fail to be interesting to the student of our early dramatic literature. " It may be objected (says Heywood, in his ' General History of Women,' 1624) why, amongst sad and grave histories, I have here and there inserted fabulous tales and jests, savouring of lightness. — I answer, I have therein imitated our historical and comical poets that write to the stage; who, lest the auditory should be dulled with serious courses, which are merely weighty and material, in every act present some zany, with his mimic action, to breed in the less capable mirth and laughter: for they that write to all must strive to please all."

Many of the anecdotes or incidents in the following pages will strike all readers as merely puerile and absurd; and they will be disposed to wonder how our ancestors could find entertainment in displays of folly and weakness, by which they themselves were not unfrequently sufferers. We must throw our imaginations back two or three centuries, into the state of society then prevailing in this country, or we shall be disposed to think, that those who laughed at and relished such scenes were little less far gone in fatuity than the principal agent in them. To the readers of the day when the work was written it must have been extremely welcome; and the author, no doubt truly, professes to have been an eye-witness of some of the circumstances he narrates. Thus, it seems extremely probable that he himself saw the remarkable scenes he describes at Edinburgh, in which King James and his fool were concerned; and, as he was a member of the company to which Shakespeare belonged, we may speculate that he visited the Scottish metropolis in his professional capacity, and associated with our great dramatist. We have no direct evidence to establish that Shakespeare was ever beyond the Tweed, but it is certain that some members of the company of actors to which he belonged were at one time as far north as Aberdeen; and that Laurence Fletcher, whose name stands first in the patent or licence, granted by James I. early in 1603, was complimented at Aberdeen by the freedom of the city.

It is enough to make us take a strong interest about Robert Armin, to know that he was one of the original performers in Shakespeare's plays, and that his name is inserted in the list of actors which follows the dedication by Heminge and Condell of the folio of 1623. Of the nature of the characters he sustained we have no precise information; but, in the preliminary matter to one of his productions ("The Italian Tailor and his Boy," 4to., 1609), he

INTRODUCTION. ix

quotes a part of the language of Dogberry, telling his patron and patroness, Lord and Lady Haddington, that he had been " writ down an ass in his time," as if quoting from one of his known parts. However, it seems certain that Kemp and Cowley were the original Dogberry and Verges of " Much Ado about Nothing," for both in the 4to and in the folio their names, instead of the names of the characters, are inserted at the head of the scenes in which the constable and his companion appear.[a]

[a] We may take this opportunity of correcting Mr. Knight on a point regarding which he has fallen into an error both in his "Pictorial" and in his "Library Shakspere," from not having consulted the earlier editions of the plays. "There is," he observes, "*a remarkable peculiarity in the text of the folio*, which indicates very clearly that it was printed from a playhouse copy * * * In the third act, when the two inimitable guardians of the night first descend upon the solid earth in Messina, to move mortals for ever after with unextinguishable laughter, they speak to us in their well-known names of Dogberry and Verges; but in the fourth we find the names of mere human actors prefixed to what they say: Dogberry becomes Kempe, and Verges Cowley. Here, then, we have *a piece of the prompter's book* before us." Mr. Knight's inference fails him, because what he notices as " a remarkable peculiarity " in the folio of 1623, derived from " the prompter's book," is common both to the folio of 1623 and to the 4to of 1600. The folio of 1623 was, in fact, printed precisely from the 4to of 1600, with the names of Kemp and Cowley instead of those of Dogberry and Verges. Mr. Knight would, of course, not have committed this mistake had he resorted to a copy of the 4to 1600. He adds, that Heminge and Condell permitted the names of Kemp and Cowley to remain as they found them in the prompter's book " as a historical tribute to the memory of their fellows." If there were any tribute to Kemp and Cowley, it was paid by Valentine Simmes, the printer of the 4to 1600, who perpetuated a blunder he found in the manuscript from which " Much Ado about Nothing" was composed by the men in his employ.

We have reason to know that, not long after the publication of "Much Ado about Nothing," Kemp left the company of the king's players, and joined those of Prince Henry (a point to which we shall presently more distinctly advert); and possibly Armin succeeded to some of the comic parts, which Kemp had previously represented. Moreover, it appears that Armin was at first instructed in the quality of a player by the celebrated Richard Tarlton, who was most famous as, what we now call, a low comedian, though at least one authority may be quoted to shew that he was also a distinguished tragic performer.[b] In an epigram inserted by John Davies of Hereford in his "Scourge of Folly," Armin is termed "honest gameson Armin;" and, on the whole, we may

[b] We allude to Stradling's Epigram, published in his "Epigrammatum Libri Quatuor," Londini, 1607. 12mo.

RICH. TARLTONO, COMŒDORUM PRINCIPI.

"Cujus, viator, sit sepulchrum hoc scire vis,
  Inscriptionem non habens?
Asta, gradumque siste paulisper tuum:
  Incognitum nomen scies.
Princeps Comœdorum tulit quos Angliæ
  Tellus, in hoc busto cubat.
Quo mortuo, spretæ silent comediæ,
  Tragediæque turbidæ.
Scenæ decus desiderant mutæ suum,
  Risusque abest Sardonius.
Hic Roscius Britannicus sepultus est,
  Quo notior nemo fuit.
Abi, viator: Sin te adhuc nomen latet,
  Edicet hoc quivis puer."

This epigram is quoted at length in "The Archæologist," No. I. p. 27, and, we think, elsewhere.

INTRODUCTION.

conclude that the line of characters he usually filled was of a humorous and ludicrous description.

We have mentioned that he was a pupil of Tarlton. This fact we have upon the evidence of the volume of Jests published in the name of that comic performer, of which the earliest known edition bears date in 1611: it was again printed in 1638—at least, a copy with that date is among Malone's books at Oxford; but how often it had been reprinted in the interval between 1611 and 1638 it is impossible to decide. Neither could the edition of 1611 have been by any means the first; for Tarlton died in 1588, and three-and-twenty years could not have been allowed to elapse before such a collection of stories, relating to so popular an actor, was put to press. At what date Armin received instructions from Tarlton we have no information; but Armin was then an apprentice, and therefore certainly quite young. The story is this:—that Armin, being apprenticed to a goldsmith, was sent to an inn in Gracechurch Street to receive payment for a bill: there he met with Tarlton, who took a fancy to him, induced him to quit his trade, and to take to the stage as a means of obtaining a livelihood. In order to qualify Armin for the profession, Tarlton took him for some time under his own tuition;—that is to say, in all probability, he engaged Armin as his boy— for nearly all the principal actors of that day and afterwards had boys under them, whom they taught to play, and who, when properly qualified, and until their beards grew, usually sustained female characters.

We must suppose Armin to have been not less than fourteen or fifteen years old, when he became acquainted with Tarlton; and, as he appeared in print as early as 1590, we can scarcely imagine that he took to the stage later than about 1580. It is singular to see the name of an actor in connection with a work entitled, " A brief Resolution of the right Religion :" such, however, is the fact; but all that Armin did was to write a preliminary prose address in commendation of the work, and, possibly, the author was induced to solicit his name in consequence of its popularity.[c]

It is generally believed that Tarlton principally exhibited at the Curtain in Shoreditch; but that theatre was not built until about 1575, and he was certainly an applauded actor before that date. He was the author of a ballad printed in 1570, and must have put his name to it, not from any vanity of authorship on account of the merit of the production itself, but because it was thought that it would give it a considerable sale : it was upon the floods in Bedfordshire and Lincolnshire, in the year we have mentioned, and it may be found printed from the original broadside in the first publication issued by the Percy Society.[d] After the death of Tarlton, Armin perhaps took some of his master's parts, and lent his name in a manner somewhat similar.

[c] The title-page runs thus: " A Briefe resolution of the right Religion, touching the controversies that are now in England. Written by C. S. London. Printed by Roger Ward for John Proctor, &c. 1590. 8vo." Armin's contribution to this work does not contain a syllable about himself.

[d] It is called " A very lamentable and wofull Discours of the fierce Fluds, which lately flowed in Bedford shire, in Lincoln shire, and in many other places, with the great losses of sheep and other cattel, the 5 of October, 1570."

About this date, or a little afterwards, Armin must have been a writer of some celebrity, for Thomas Nash, in his " Strange News," 1592, mentions him in company with Thomas Deloney, Philip Stubbs, &c., as one of the progeny of " their father Elderton," the notorious ballad-maker. Nash associated Stubbs with them for the purpose of derogating from his reputation as the author of " The Anatomy of Abuses," which, having been first published in 1583, went through several editions before 1592. Nothing by Armin, or attributed to him, of this date has survived. All evidence tends to shew that by far the greater part of the ephemeral literature of that period has perished. It was not usually in a form calculated for preservation; and, even where it assumed a more respectable and permanent shape, as in the tract hereafter reprinted, it was so handed about from one reader to another, and so carelessly and unceremoniously treated by all readers, that it is almost a wonder that a single copy has descended to us. Such prolific penmen as Elderton, Deloney, Johnson, and others, would smile if they could see the eagerness with which their productions are now purchased, and the chariness with which they are treasured in the portfolios of our curious collectors, who have often given more pounds for a copy of a ballad, than the writer of it received pence for composing it.

We hear nothing more of Armin, either as author or actor, until we find his name among the company licensed by James I. when he came to the throne, and thereafter called " the King's Majesty's Players." If any thing be to be inferred from the fact, it may be noticed that his name stands last but one in the list of nine players, including Lawrence Fletcher and Shakespeare, who are at the head of the company.

Nevertheless, a circumstance occurred in the next year which may lead us to believe that Armin was then in considerable favour with the public. At this date he must have been upon the stage more than twenty years; but, as before remarked, the retirement of Kemp from the company might again give Armin a temporary prominence as the successor to such parts as Dogberry, Peter, Launcelot, or Touchstone. Had Kemp not retired previous to the 17th of May, 1603, it is strange, considering his eminence in the profession, that his name should not have been mentioned in the patent; but we have positive testimony in Henslowe's Diary that he had withdrawn, and had enlisted himself in the rival association led by Edward Alleyn—the Players of Prince Henry. There are numerous entries relating to Kemp, and to dresses furnished to him for his different characters, and to money advanced to him in the spring, summer, and autumn of 1602; the earliest bears date on the 10th March of that year, when Henslowe lent William Kemp twenty shillings; another comparatively small sum was advanced to him on the 22nd August, 1602, and a third entry of a loan is found under the date of the 3rd of September following. This fact is a novelty in the life of this performer, and the Rev. Mr. Dyce was not acquainted with it, when he drew up the excellent memoir which precedes the reprint, under the sanction of the Camden Society, of "Kemp's Nine Days' Wonder," 4to 1600. Neither is it of small importance with reference to some of Shakespeare's dramas; for, if Kemp ceased to belong to the King's Players, he could not have been the performer of parts assigned to him in pieces which were produced after he quitted the company. We may take this opportunity of mentioning, as an incidental circumstance, that Kemp was still alive, and still acting, in 1605. We afterwards hear no more of him, and possibly he died of the plague, which prevailed to a fearful extent in that year.

Our reason for thinking that Armin was a popular actor in 1604 is, that, in that year, he wrote an introductory epistle to a small tract penned by Gilbert Dugdale (whom Armin terms " his kinsman," and who was the author of a pageant on the coronation of James I.), under the following title: " A true Discourse of the Practises of Elizabeth Caldwell, Ma. Jeffrey Bownd, Isabell Hall widdow, and George Ferneby, on the parson of Ma. Thomas Caldwell, in the County of Chester, to haue murdered and poysoned him with divers others, &c. At London, printed by James Roberts for John Busbie, &c. 1604." 4to. Armin's epistle comes immediately after the title-page, and as it relates mainly to himself, and as the tract in which it is found is of rare occurrence, we subjoin it.

"To the right honourable and his singular good Lady, the Lady Mary Chandois,

" R. A. wisheth health and everlasting happinesse.

"My honourable and very good Lady, considering my duty to your kind Ladyship, and remembring the vertues of your prepared minde, I could doe noe lesse but dedicate this strange worke to your view, being both matter of moment and truth. And to the whole world it may seem strange that a gentlewoman so well brought vp in God's feare, so well married, so vertuous ever, so suddenly wrought to this act of murder; that when your Ladiship doth read as well the Letter as the Booke of her owne indighting, you will the more wonder that her vertues coulde so aptly tast the follies of vice and villanie. But so it was; and, for the better proofe that it was so, I haue placed my kinsman's name to it, who was present at all her troubles, at her comming to prison, her beeing in prison, and her going out of prison to execution. That, those Gentlemen to whom he dedicates his worke witnessed, may also be pertakers in that kind, for the proofe thereof, that your Ladiship and the world, so satisfied, may admire the deede, and hold it as strange as it is true.

"We have many giddie-pated poets, that coulde have published the report with more eloquence; but truth, in plaine attire, is the easier knowne: let fixion maske in Kendall greene. It is my qualitie to add to the truth, truth, and not leasings to lyes.

"Your good honor knowes *Pinck's* poor heart, who, in all my services to your late deceased kind lord, neuer sauoured of flatterie or fixion: and, therefore, am now the bolder to present to your vertues the view of this late truth, desiring you to so think of it that you may be an honourable mourner at these obsequies, and you shall no more doe than manie more haue doone. So with my tendered dutie, my true ensuing storie, and my euer wishing well, I do humbly commit your Ladiship to the prison of heauen, wherein is perfect freedome.

"Your Ladiships euer
"In duty and seruice,
"ROBERT ARMIN."

How Armin acquired the nickname of Pink, and in what capacity he had been in the service of the husband of the lady he addresses, we are left to conjecture: it is very likely that Lord Chandos, like many other noblemen, had at one time a company of theatrical retainers in his pay and under his patronage, and that Armin had been one of them.

His next work, at least the next regarding which we

have any information, was that now presented to the members of the Shakespeare Society. On the personal matter it contains, it is, therefore, unnecessary to dwell. We may observe that it is not mentioned in "The Bibliographer's Manual," by Lowndes, and that the only catalogue of books in which we have seen it included is that of Malone at Oxford, where, as already stated, the sole remaining copy is deposited. From it our transcript has been made. The tract was evidently hastily and carelessly printed for a bookseller who published many humorous works, and the errors of the press, especially in the later sheets, are numerous, and in some places not easy of correction.

We apprehend that Armin was, at this date, struggling with poverty, and that he wrote "The Nest of Ninnies" mainly to supply his necessities. Such was certainly the case with his next production, which came out in the following year, 1609. It was called "The Italian Taylor and his Boy," and is a translation, in verse, of novel 5, night viii. of the *Notti Piacevoli* of Straparola. Armin acknowledges it to be from the Italian, though he does not add the name of his author. On the title-page he still states himself to be "Servant to the king's most excellent Majesty;" and no doubt he yet belonged to the company, though an actor of, perhaps, thirty years' standing. In the preliminary matter he more than once confesses his poverty, and that he wrote the tract in hopes of raising money : we may therefore presume that he had, at this date, but a very small, or perhaps no share as proprietor in the Globe and Blackfriars theatres, for which Shakespeare was writing in the plenitude of his popularity, and which must then have been profitable undertakings.

In his address *Ad lectorem hic et ubique*, before " The Italian Taylor and his Boy," Armin speaks of his " Nest of Ninnies," which had been printed in the year preceding; and the dedication to Lord and Lady Haddington contains the following interesting mention of a poet of considerable celebrity, who had been the early friend of Spenser, to whom Chapman dedicated his " Shadow of Night," in 1594, who was living in retirement in 1609, and who was in such distress, not many years afterwards, that he was glad to accept from Edward Alleyn, the founder of Dulwich College, very trifling charitable donations.

" There is (says Armin to Lady Haddington) under the glister of your starre a poetical light, which shines not in the world as it is wisht, but yet the worth of its lustre is known : he hath remayned in Sussex many yeares ; and I beseech God and your noble Father (the Earle) he may live and die beloued so still. It is (if I speake darkely) that pen-pleading poet (graue for yeares and knowledge) Maister Mathew Roiden : I doe stand to his censure, to second yours both ; and I doubt not but he will plead for my weaknes in this worke, knowing that *Non cuivis homini contingit adire Corinthum.*"

The Earl of Fitzwalter, the father of Lady Haddington, did not die until 1629 ; but, some years before that event, Matthew Roiden, or Roydon, must have been reduced to extreme want : he was relieved by Alleyn in 1618 by the gift of eightpence, and in 1622 he made another appeal to his charity, and obtained sixpence. (See "Memoirs of Alleyn," p. 155.)

In the same year that " The Italian Taylor and his Boy" came out, Armin printed a dramatic piece, with the title of "The History of the Two Maids of More Clacke, with the Life and simple manners of John in the Hospital." It purports to have been acted by the Children of the King's Revels, although Armin, as the title-page asserts, was "Servant to the King's most excellent Majesty." Whether he was alive in 1615 does not appear, but in that year was published another play called "The Valiant Welchman," the plot of which the Editor of the Biographia Dramatica gravely informs us was taken from Milton's History of England, which was, of course, not published until many years afterwards. The initials "R. A. Gent" only are upon the title-page of "The Valiant Welshman," and it may be doubted whether Armin had any concern in the authorship of it. It was reprinted in 1663.

The following tract will be found to contain the names of several fools and jesters not elsewhere commemorated. The most celebrated in the list is William Somer, Sommers, or Summers, the favourite of Henry VIII., who figures in, at least, two plays of the time of Shakespeare —Thomas Nash's "Summers Last Will and Testament," acted in 1593, and printed in 1600; and Samuel Rowley's "When you see me you know me," founded upon incidents in the life and reign of Henry VIII., acted about 1604, and printed in 1605. He was a jester of a different character to the others, inasmuch as he was an artificial fool—a witty person, affecting simplicity for the sake of affording amusement. Jesters of this class were often entertained in families where mere idiots would not have been tolerated; but they had their origin in the license allowed to the tongues of "innocents," as they were sometimes, for the sake of distinction, called. William Sommers was a historical personage, and is so treated by Samuel Rowley in his play, which is a singular picture of manners, and of the mode in which, just after the death of Elizabeth, her father was exhibited at the public theatres. In this view, " When you see me you know me" may be said to have a direct relation to the "Henry the Eighth" of our great dramatist, and may well deserve to be hereafter reprinted by the Shakespeare Society.

We have to thank Mr. Thoms for some very useful notes, which are distinguished from the rest by his initials.

J. P. C.

A

NEST OF NINNIES

Simply of themselves without Compound.

Stultorum plena sunt omnia.

BY ROBERT ARMIN.

LONDON:
Printed by T. E. for Iohn Deane. 1608.

To the most true and rightly compleat in all good gifts and graces, the generous gentlemen of Oxenford, Cambridge, and the Innes of Court. Ro. Armin greeting.

> You first borne brothers of the highest skies,
> Twins of best Joue by blest Memoria,
> From whom our glories and our liuings rise;
> Brothers and sonnes to him that brings the day
> (Phœbus) whom none can see but by your eyes;
> You only, and you euer I shall pray,
> And praysing euer that your sunnie shine
> May beautifie our GLOBE in euery line.

But what higher straine am I in, when your selues haue set my tongue lower?

Most liberall and well affected, I am brazed by your fauours, made bould in your ostended curtesies, I haue seene you both wayes, as the hare that squints on either side—marry to looke fore-right I cannot, because judgement out-lookes mee. But as the philosopher squened at his curst wife in some feare, because of quiet, so I, fearefull, presume not to look into the milstone, least I grauell my eye sight. I haue seene the stars at midnight in your societies, and might have commenst, like an asse as I was; but I lackt liberty in that, yet I was admitted in Oxford to be of Christs Church, while they of Al-soules gaue ayme: such as knew me remember my measures. I promised them to proue mad; and I thinke I am so, else I would not meddle with folly so deepely, but similis similem,

&c. If I doe offend, as I make no question, my pardon is signed, I doubt not—marry there is an execution yet behinde, and I long till I passe my plundge, that is censure. They say he goes in collours, as one strangely affected, and I goe in motly, making my own cloakebag ready. If hee proue porter, and beare with me, I shall rest behoulding; if not, I am his martir, and suffer extreamly. I haue, gentlemen, in this booke gone through Ireland; if I doe sticke in the bogs, help me out—not with your good skene head me; that's the way to spoyle all, but with your goad pricke me on the true tract. And you of our Innes of Court, nimble braind brands that burne without smoking, I challenge of you neighbourly neerenesse, and therefore dare say sumus in toto. If you should flie out like rancke riders, or rebell like the Irish, twere much, because my presumption challenges better being in you. But since all is one, and one all that's car'd for, singlenesse hath such regard, I make a question, which if you easily answere I am satisffied, otherwise buryed quicke: how euer, my loue looses not his labour—an universitie fire in the winter, and a temple pot may warme good licour, in which you may drink to me, and ile pledge you. I may liue to make you amends, if not no more but this — such a one died in your debt, and thats a countertenor many a one sings. Vale, as far vide and vici let Cæsar at his next arriue, so salute you.

Yours euer affected,
RO. ARMIN.

A NEST OF NINNIES.

The World, wanton sick, as one surfetting on sinne (in morning pleasures, noone banquets, after riots, night moriscoes, midnights modicoms, and abundance of trash trickt up to all turbulent reuellings) is now leaning on her elbow, deuising what doctour may deliuer her, what phisicke may free her, and what antidotes may antissipate so dangerous a dolemma: shee now begins to grow bucksome as a lightning before death; and, gad, she will — riches, her chamberlaine, could not keepe her in; beauty, her bed-fellow, was bold to perswade her; and sleepy securitie, mother of all mischiefe— tut, her prayers was but meere prattle: out she would, tucks up her trinkets, like a Dutch tannikin sliding to market on the ise, and away she flings—and whither thinck you?—

> Not to the Law, that was too loud—
> Not to the Church, that was too proud.
> Not to the Court, that was too stately—
> Nor to the Cittie, she was there lately.
> Nor to the Campe, that was to keene—
> No, nor to the Country, where seldom seene—

shee daines her a friendly eye; but, of all, into a philosophers cell, who, because he was alwayes poking at Fortune with his forefinger, the wise wittely namde him Sotto, as one besotted —a grumbling sir; one that was wise enough, and fond enough, and solde all for a glasse prospective, because he would wisely see into all men but himselfe, a fault generall in most; but such was his, who thus busied, was tooke napping by the weale publike, who smiles upon him with a wapper eye, a iealous countenance, and bids him all haile! Mistresse (sayes Sotto) I will not say welcome, because you come ill to him that would bee alone ; but, since you are come, looke for such entertainement as my folly fits you with, that is, sharp sauce with bitter dyet ; no swetnes at al, for that were to mingle your pils with sugar : no, I am all one, winter in the head, and frost in the foot ; no summer in me but my smiles, and that as soone gone as smiles. The bauble I play with is mens estates, which I so tumble from hand to hand, that, weary with it, I see (gluttingly and grieuedly, yet mingled with smiles too) in my glasse prospectiue what shall become of it. The World, curling her locks with her fingers, and anone scratching her braine with her itching pin, as one little regarding, answeres, What then? Marry, sayes Hodge, ile show thee. See, World, in whose bosome euer hath abundance beene poured, what thy imps of impiety bee ; for as they (I) all for the most part, as these which I will present to thee in my glasse prospectiue : mark them well, and see what thou breedest in thy wantonnesse, sixe children like thee, not the father that begat them—Where were they nursed? in folly : fed with the flottin milke of nicetie and wantonnesse, curdled in thy wombe of water and bloud, vnseasoned, because thy mother bearing temper was euer vntrue, farre from the rellish of right breede ; and it is hard that the taste of one apple should distaste the whole lumpe of this defused chaios. But marke me and my glasse : see into some (and in them thy selfe) whom I haue discride, or describde, these sixe parts of folly in thee ; thou shalt see them as cleare as day, how mistic thy clouds be, and what rancknesse raines from them.

The World, queasie stomackt, as one fed with the earth's nectar and delicates, with the remembrance of her own appetite, squinies at this, and lookes as one scorning ; yet beholding what will follow, at length espies a tall blacke man, jearing like himselfe, a foole in motley, muckinder hunge, euer and anon wipes his nose; at whose girdle hangde a small black jack of a quart, his vsual draft; his finger on his tongue, as if he blamde Nature that cut not the strings of it in more large manner, but hindred by defect, hee still did gesse at wisedome, though seldome attaining it. Well, he was gouty, bigge, poste legged, and of yeeres something many, as in the right sequell followeth :—

> This foole was tall, his face small,
> His beard was big and blacke;
> His necke was short, inclind to sport,
> Was this our dapper Jack.
> Of nature curst, yet not the worst,
> Was nastie, giuen to sweare;
> Toylesome euer, his endeauour
> Was delight in beare.
> Goutie, great, of conceit
> Apt, and full of fauor;
> Curst, yet kinde, and inclinde
> To spare the wise mans labour.
> Knowne to many, loude of any,
> Cause his trust was truth;
> Seene in toyes, apt to joyes.
> To please with tricks of youth;
> Writh'd i'th knees, yet who sees
> Faults that hidden be?
> Calfe great, in whose conceit
> Lay much game and glee.
> Bigge i'th small, ancle all,
> Footed broad and long;
> In motly cotes, goes Jacke Oates,
> Of whom I sing this song.

The World, ready to disgorge at so homely a present, askt if it were possible such breathde hers to commaunde? Oh, saith our philosophicall Hodge, beare his iests, and what an vnknowne habite liues in him, then returne iudgement. Marke our application.

Jack Oates, sitting at cardes all alone, was dealing to himselfe at vide ruffe (for that was the game he ioyed in) and as he spide a knaue—Ah, knaue, art there? quoth he. When he spide a king—King, by your leaue, quoth he. If hee spied a queene—Queene Richard art come? quoth he; and would kneele downe, and bid God blesse her majestie (meaning, indeede, the then queene, whom he heard Sir William Hollis, his maister, so much to pray for). But heere is the jest: Jack, as I say, being at cardes all alone, spying a knaue, and saying, Ah, knaue, art there? a simple seruingman being in the hall, waighting his maisters comming, walking by, and hearing him say so, thought he had called him knaue, tooke the matter in dudgeen, and miscalled the foole. Another seruingman, more foolish then both, took Jack's part, so that in short time they two fell together by the eares; who, being parted, Jack Oates giues them each one a hand, and so takes them into the buttry to drinke. The knight comes in: seeing the hall not yet quiet, askt the matter. Jack comes—Ile tell thee, Willy, quoth hee. As I was a playing at cardes, one seeing I wonne all I playd for, would needes haue the knaue from mee, which, as very a knaue as hee seeing, would needes beare him knaue for company; so bid them both welcome to thy house—I haue bin to intreat the knaue, thy butler, to make them drinke. I, sayes Sir William; and you, like a knaue, made them fall out. I, answered Jack, and your drinke, Sir Knaue, made them friends. Sir William, laughing, departed.

Newes came to Sir William that such a nobleman was comming to his house: great prouision was made for his welcome; and, amongst all, Jack Oates put on his new motly coate, cleane muckender, and his new shooes. Much preparation was made, which were too long to tell; for, Ile assure ye, it was one of the greatest earles in England, vnfit to name here: but the knight and his ladie met him at the gate to entertaine him. Sir William, with a low congy, saluted him; the good lady, as is the courtly custom, was kist of this noble man. Jack Oates, seeing him kisse his ladie, on the sodaine giues the earle a sound box on the eare. Knaue (quoth he) kisse Sir Willie's wife? The good knight, amazed at this, caused him to be whipt. But the kinde noble man, knowing simplicitie the ground of his errour, would not suffer it, but, putting it vp, left him, and entred the house. Jack, seeing they were sad, and he had done amisse, had this wit in simplicitie to shadow it: he comes after and askt the earle wher his hand was? Here (quoth he)—with that he shakes him by it, and sayes, I mistooke it before, knowing not your eare from your hand, being so like one another. Jack thought hee had mended the matter; but now he was whipt indeede, and had his payment altogether. Thus fooles, thinking to be wise, become flat foolish: but all is one, Jack neuer repented him.

At a Christmas time, when great logs furnish the hall fire—when brawne is in season, and, indeede, all reveling is regarded, this gallant knight kept open house for all commers, where beefe, beere, and bread was no niggard. Amongst all the pleasures prouided, a noyse of minstrells and a Lincolnshire bagpipe was prepared — the minstrels for the great chamber, the bagpipe for the hall—the minstrells to serue vp the knights meate, and the bagpipe for the common dauncing. Jack could not endure to bee in the common hall; for, indeede, the foole was a little proudly minded, and, therefore, was altogether in the great chamber, at my ladies or Sir Williams elbow. One time, being very melancholy, the knight, to rouse him vp, saide, Hence, foole! Ile haue another foole; thou shalt dwell no longer with me. Jack to this answered little; though, indeede, ye could not anger him worse. A gentleman at the boord answers, If it please you, sir, Ile bring ye another foole soone. I pray ye do (quoth the knight) and he shall be welcome. Jack fell a crying, and departed mad and angry down into the great hall; and, being strong armed (as before I described him), caught the bagpipes from the piper, knockt them about his pate, that he laid the fellow for dead on the ground, and, all broken, carries the pipes vp into the great chamber, and layes them on the fire. The knight, knowing by Jack that something was amisse, sendes downe to see. Newes of this jest came; the knight, angry (but to no purpose, for he loued the foole aboue all, and that the household knew, else Jack had paid for it, for the common peoples dauncing was spoiled) sent downe Jack, and bad him out of his sight. Jack cries, Hang Sir Willy, hang Sir Willy, and departes.

Sir William, not knowing how to amend the matter, caused the piper to be carried to bed, who was very ill, and said, I would now giue a gold noble for a foole: indeede, to anger him throughly, one of the minstrels whispers a gentleman in the eare, and said, If it pleased him, hee would; whereat the gentleman laught. The knight demaunded the reason of his laughing. I pray you tell me (quoth hee)—for laughing could neuer come in a better time — the foole hath madded me. If it please you (sayes the gentleman), here is a good fellow will goe and attire him in one of his coates, and can in all poynts behaue himselfe naturally, like such a one. It is good (sayes the knight) and I prethee, good fellow, about it; and one goe call Jack Oates hether, that wee may hold him with talk in the meane time.

The simple minstrell, thinking to worke wonders, as one ouerjoyed at the good opportunitie, threw his fiddle one way, his stick another, and his case the third way, and was in such a case of joy, that it was no boot to bid him make hast: but, proud of the knights fauor, away he flings, as if he went to tak possession of some great lordship; but, what ere he got by it, I am sure his fiddle, with the fall, fell in pieces, which grieued his maister so, that, in loue and pittie, he laughed till the water ran downe his cheekes. Beside, this good knight was like to keepe a bad Christmas, for the bagpipes and the musicke went to wracke—the one burnt, and the other broken.

In comes Jack Oates, and (being merry) told the knight and the rest that a country-wench in the hall had eaten garlicke, and there was seuenteene men poysoned with kissing her: for it was his vse to jest thus. By and by comes in a messenger (one of the knights men) to tell him that such a gentleman had sent his foole to dwell with him. Hee is welcome, sayes the knight, for I am weary of this foole: goe bid him come in —Jack, bid him welcome. They all laught to see Jack's colour come and goe, like a wise man ready to make a good end. What say you to this? saies the knight. Not one word sayes Jack. They tinged with a knife at the bottome of a glasse, as toulling the bell for the foole, who was speechlesse and would dye (then which nothing could more anger him); but now the thought of the new come foole so much moued him, that he was as dead as a doore nayle—standing on tip-toe, looking toward the door to behold ariuall, that he would put his nose out of joint.

By and by enters my artificiall foole in his old cloaths, making wry mouthes, dauncing, and looking a squint: who, when Jack beheld, sodainely he flew at him, and so violently beate him, that all the table rose, but could scarce get him off. Well, off he was at length: the knight caused the broken ones to be by themselues. My poore minstrell, with a fall, had his head broke to the skull against the ground, his face scratcht; that which was worst of all his left eye put out, and withall so sore bruised, that he could neyther stand nor goe. The knight caused him to bee laide with the pyper, who was also hurt in the like conflict, who lackt no good looking to, because they miscarried in the knights seruice: but euer after Jack Oates could not endure to heare any talke of another foole to be there, and the knight durst not make such a motion. The pyper and the minstrel, being in bed together, one cryed, O! his backe and face; the other, O! his face and eye: the one cryed O his pype! the other, O his fiddle! Good mussicke or broken consorts, they agree well together; but when they were well, they were contented for their paines: they had both money and the knights fauour. Here you haue heard the difference twixt a flat foole naturall, and a flat foole artificiall; one that did his kinde, and the other who foolishly followed his owne minde: on which two is written this Rime:—

> Naturall fooles are prone to selfe conceipt:
> Fooles artificiall, with their wits lay wayte
> To make themselues fooles, liking the disguise,
> To feede their owne mindes, and the gazers eyes.
> Hee that attempts daunger, and is free,
> Hurting himselfe, being well, cannot see,
> Must with the fidler, heere, weare the fooles coates,
> And bide his pennance sign'd him by Jack Oates.
> All such, say I, that use flat foolerie,
> Beare this, beare more; this flat foole's companie.

Jack Oates could neuer abide the cooke, by reason that he would scald him out of the kitchen. Upon a time he had a great charge from his Lady to make her a quince pie of purpose for Sir Williams owne eating, which the cooke endeuored to doe, and sent to Lincolne of purpose to the apothecaries for choyse quinces. Jack, being at this charge giuen, thought to be euen with the cooke, and waited the time when this Pie was made. It hapned so, the cooke could get no quinces: my lady (for it was the knight's desire to haue one) sent about to Boston, and all the chiefe townes, but all in vaine — the season serued not; but, rather then Sir William should be vnfurnished, sent to Lincolne againe to buy vp many quinces, ready preserved at pothecaries, which she had, though with great cost. The knight, asking his Lady for his pie, she told him with much adoe she had preuailed, but with no little paines, in seeking quinces; for she was faine to buy them ready preserued, and to make a vertue of necessity that way. Sir William, seeing it was so, said it should bee as well eaten, and sent for his friends, gentlemen and others of no small account. There was other great cheare prouided to furnish vp this sumptuous feast, and as he inuited them, hee tolde them it was a quince pie, which he would haue eaten. The day drew on, and the gentiles were come, and all was in a redinesse, and still Jack forgat not the pie, but stood faintly sicke, and refused his meate: the knight, sory that his best dish fayled him, made no small account of his well fare, askte him, Jack, sayes hee, where lyes thy paine? In my mouth, sayes hee (meaning, indeede, his mouth hung for the quince pie.) A barber was sent for from a market towne hard by, who searcht his mouth, and could finde no cause of paine: but Sir William, thinking the foole wanted wit to tell his griefe (though not wit to play the thiefe) had the barber depart, asking Jacke what he would eate? he sayd, nothing. What he would drinke? he sayd, nothing; which made Sir William doubt much of his health, refusing his liquour when it was usually his practice, and the knight joyed in it too: askit him if he would lie downe? still answering no, but would stand by the kitchen fire. The knight, that never came there but he did some exployte, forgetting that, led him by the hand (so much he made of him) and bad the cooke see he wanted nothing. Jack, standing still, groan'd and sayd, If he dyed, he would forgive all the world but the cooke. Hang, foole, (sayes the cooke) I care not for thee: die to-morrow if thou wilt, and so followed his business. They knockt to the dresser, and the dinner went up. Jack had a sheepes eye in the oven: anone the second course came, the pie was drawne, set by, and among other backt meates was to be sent up; but, wanting sugar, stept aside to the spicerie to fetch it; and Jack, in the meantime, catcheth the pie and claps it under his coate, and so runs through the hall into the yard, where was a broade moate: and, as he ran, the hot pie burned his belly. I, sayes Jack, are ye so hot, Sir Willies pie? Ile quence ye anone Sir Willies pie, sayes he; and straight, very subtilly, leapes into the moate up to the arm-pits, and there stood eating the pie. The cooke comes in, misses the pie, withal misses Jack, cryes out, The pie! Sir Williams pie was gone, the author of that feast was gone, and they all were undone. A hurly burly went through the house, and one comes and whispers the lady with the newes: she tels Sir William how Jack Oates had stolen the pie. Jack was searcht for, and anon found in the moate. It was told the knight where the foole was eating it. Gentlemen (quoth he) we are disfurnished of our feast; for Jack, my foole, is in my moate, up to the arme-pits, eating of the pie. They laught, and ran to the windows to see the jest: then they might see Jack eate, the cooke call, the people hallow, but to no purpose. Jack fed, and, feeding greedily, (more to anger the cooke, than disapoint Sir William) ever as he burnt his mouth with hast, dipt the pie in the water to coole it. O! sayes the cooke, it is Sir William's owne pie, sirra. O! sayes Jack hang thee and Sir Willy too: I care not; it is mine now. Save Sir William some, sayes one; save my lady some, sayes another. By James, not a bit, sayes Jack; and eate up all, to the wonder of the beholders, who never knew him eate so much before, but drink ten times more. At length out comes Jack dropping dry, and goes to get fire to dry him: the knight and the rest all laught a good at the jest: not knowing how to amend it, Sir William sends for the cooke, who came up with a sorrowful heart, and, lamentably complaining, said it was the knights fault for placing him in the kitchen, where he never was but hee did like villany. The knight, not satisfied with the cookes answere, presently discharges him of his service, and sent him to live elsewhere. Goe, sayes he; trusse up your trinkets and be gone. The cooke, seeing no remedy, departed.

Jack, being dry, up he comes; and, knowing he had offended,

tels a jest (for it was his manner so to doe) how a yong man brake his codpiece point, and let all be seene that God sent him, or such fooleries, but that was not enough; and to chide him was to make of things worse then 'twas, and to no purpose neither. Sir William demaunded why hee eate the pye? Because I had a stomacke, sayes Jack. Would nought else serve, sayes the knight, but my pye? No, Willy, sayes he, thou would not be angry then, and the cooke had not been turned away: but all is well — thou art rich enough to buy more. The knight, perceiving the fooles envie, sent for the cooke, and bid him enjoy his place againe. So all parties [were] well pleased but the yong big-bellied woman, who, perchance, longed for this long looked for pie; but if she did, though long lookt for comes at last, yet they shoote short that ayme to hit this marke, for Jack Oates had eaten the pie and served himselfe. This was a flat foole; yet, now and then, a blind man may hit a crow, and you know a fooles boult is soone shot: out it goes, happen how it will. Had Jack kept his owne counsell, the cooke had beene still out of service, and [he] had been revenged, but now, being in his place againe, may live to cry quittance for the quince pye.

These, quoth the World, are pretty toyes. I, quoth the philosopher, but marke the applyance. By Jack Oates is morrally meant many described like him; though not fooles naturall, yet most artificiall: they carde hence what their parents spin, and doe such apish tricks, that rapine, ruine, and a thousand inconveniences, follow. By the knight is meant maintainers of foolery: by the hall, the inne where the cards of vanity causeth many to be bewitcht; as appears in the serving men, who, busie in others braules, are as easily made friends, as they were set together by the ears. By the second is meant [those who] reach at stars, ayming at honour, lighting sometime on the eare of memory, but ill taken because badly meant—is rewarded with a deserved whipping. By the third is called to question most that musically fret their time out in idle baubling, and will become artificiall fooles to outbraue fooles indeede, but stick often in their owne quick-sands, and are got out with repentance. But the fourth and last shews the deuouring of deuoutions dyet: how euer come by, yet they will stand up to the arme-pits in daunger rather than to lack their wills, to slacke or rebate the edge of their appetites. With this the World, a little humde and haide, said shee was not pleased that such liued, and did promise some amendment, but desired to see further.

Now our philosophical poker pokte on, and poynted to a strange shew; the fat foole, not so tall, but this fat foole as low, whose description runs in meeter thus: —

> This fat foole was a Scot borne, brought vp
> In Sterlin, twenty miles from Edinborough,
> Who, being but young, was for the king caught vp;
> Ser'ud this king's father all his life time through.
> A yard high and a nayle, no more, his stature;
> Smooth fact, fayre spoken, yet vnkinde by nature.
> Two yards in compasse and a nayle, I reade,
> Was he at forty yeeres, since when I heard not
> Nor of his life or death, and further heede,
> Since I neuer read, I looke not, nor regard not.
> But what at that time Iemy Camber was,
> As I haue heard Ile write, and so let passe.
> His head was small, his hayre long on the same:
> One eare was bigger then the other farre;
> His fore-head full, his eyes shinde like a flame,
> His nose flat, and his beard small, yet grew square;
> His lips but little, and his wit was lesse,
> But wide of mouth, few teeth, I must confesse.
> His middle thicke, as I haue said before;
> Indifferent thighs and knees, but very short;
> His legs be square, a foot long and no more;
> Whose very presence made the king much sport.
> And a pearle spoone he still wore in his cap,
> To eate his meate he loued, and got by hap.

A pretty little foote, but a big hand,
On which he ever wore rings rich and good.
Backward well made as any in that land,
Though thicke; and he did come of gentle bloud :
But of his wisdome ye shall quickly heare
How this fat foole was made on every where.

The World, smiling at this rime, describing so unseemly a portackt, gaue leave to the rest, and desired greatly to be satisfied with something done, as one longing to know what so round a trust lump could performe. The poking art's maister tels his doing thus.

When the kings and nobles of Scotland had welcomed Jemy Camber to the court, (who was their countryman, borne in Sterlin, but twenty miles from Edinborough, this kings birth-towne, as Greenvich was our late queenes) they reasoned with him to understand his wit, which indeed was just none at all, yet merry and pleasing, whereat the king rejoiced: and, seeing he was so fat, caused his doctors and phisitians to minister to him; but phisick could not alter nature, and he would neuer be but a S. Vincent's turnip, thicke and round. Wherefore the doctors persuaded his grace that the purging of the sea was good for him. Well, nothing was undone that might be done to make Jemy Camber a tall, little, slender man, when yet he lookt like a Norfolke dumpling, thicke and short: well, to Leith was he sent, which is the harbour towne of such ships as arrive at Edinborough; neerer they cannot come, which is some mile from the cittie. To sea they put in a ship, at whose departure they discharged ordinance, as one that departed from the land with the kings fauour: the Earle Huntly was sent with him to sea to accompany him, so high he was esteemed with the king, who, hearing the ordinance goe off, would aske what doe they now? Marry, says the Earle, they shoot at our enemies. O, saies hee, hit, I pray God! Againe they discharge. What doe they now? quoth hee. Marry, now the

c

enimie shoots at us. O, misse, I pray God! (sayes Jemy Camber). So euer after it was a jest in the Scottish court. Hit or misse, quoth Jemy Camber; that if a maide had a barne, and did penance at the crosse, in the high towne of Edinborough, What hath shee done? did she hit or misse? She hath hit, sayes the other: better she had mist, sayes the first; and so long time after this jest was in memory—yea, I have heard it myselfe, and some will talke of it at this day. Well, to sea they put, on a faire, sunshine day, where Jemy stood fearful of every calme billow, where it was no boote to bid him tell what the ship was made of, for he did it dououtly. But see the chance: a sodaine flaw or gust rose; the winds held strong east and by west, and the ship was in great danger, insomuch as the Earle, maister and all, began to feare the weather. By and by a stronger gale blew, and split their maine-maste, and gaue their ship a mighty leake, insomuch as the crack made them all screeck out: which Jemy, hearing, was almost dead with feare. Some fell to pumping, others on their knees to praying; but the fat foole, seeing themselues in this daunger, thought there was no way but one with them, and was half dead with feare: in the end the winde turned, and the raging of the sea began to cease. I warrant thee now (quoth the maister) Jemy, wee shall not bee drowned. I, will ye warrant us? sayes the foole. I, sayes the maister, Ile giue thee my ship for thy chaine, if we bee drowned: beare witnesse, my lord, sayes hee, a plaine bargaine; and with that threw the maister his chaine, who would have given it to the Earle, but joy of their escape made him delight in the jest, and therefore the maister enjoyed his bargaine. With much adoe they attained thether againe, where the king, fearefull before, awayted their landing now; and, seeing Jemy not a jot lesse of body then hee was (onely lightened of his chaine) How now? quoth hee; how dost thou, man? O! sayes Jemy, well now, king; but till had not the maister beene, who warranted our liues for my chaine, the best bargaine that euer I made, for no way could

I haue been a looser. How? sayes the king? Marry, Ile tell thee king, quoth hee: say we had beene drowned, his ship was forfeit to me for my chaine: Earle Huntley was a witness to the bargaine; and now we are not drowned, for my chaine did warrant our liues of the maister. Nay, says the earle, not our liues; none but yours, Jemy: our liues was as safe warranted without a chaine. With this the foole had some feeling of sence, and on a sodaine cryed out mainly for his chaine, which was restored to him by the maister; but hee lost nothing by that, for he attayned to a suit, as the story sayes, that he had beene three yeeres about. Thus the king and nobles went to Edinborough, merrily talking of their feare and welfare.

Jemy, this fat foole, used every day to goe from the abbey, in the low towne by the hill, into the citie of Edinborough; and one euening, above the rest, he met with a broken virgin, one that had a barne (as there they are known by their attire) wearing a loose kerchiefe, hanging downe backward: she, I saye, cried sallets, as thus—Buy any cibus salletea? Jemy, desirous of sallets, calles her to him. Lasse, says he, what shall I giue thee for a good sallet? Faire sire, sayes the wench (for shee knew him for the kings foole, and she could not please him better then to call him faire sir) you giue me an atchison. Now he, hauing nothing but sixe French crownes about him, Canst thou change mee a crowne? sayes he. Yea, sire, sayes shee. He gives her a crowne, and shee gives him a sallet for it, and shee went her way.

Jemy thinks it was much to give a crowne for that, for which shee did demand but an atchison, which in our money is but three farthings: he runnes after and sayes, she had his fayrest crowne; but, sayes hee, giue mee that, and take your choice of these, thinking by that deuise to get the first crowne againe. Will ye chaunge? sayes the lasse: I, sayes the foole; so she takes all the fiue, and giues him one againe, and so laughing at his folly goes her way. It was in vaine to exclayme, for they will hold fast what they get; but my fat foole goes home to eate his sallet, and inuites the king to a deare dish, and made him laugh heartily at the jest. The king calls for winiger to his sallet, because his sweet meate should haue sower sauce, and perswaded him it was well bought: otherwise, if the foole had repented his bargaine, it was his manner to try for his money againe; yet, with it all, the court could not quiet him.

Betwixt Edinborough Abbey, the king's place, and Leeth, there stands an euen plaine greene meddow, in which the king used most of his sports: amongst which he rode thether one day to run at the glove, or the ring, as his grace should please. With him rides Jemy Camber on a trotting mule: it was then a maruailous hot day. O! saies Jemy, how cold the wether is (so wise was hee that hee scarce knew hot from colde). No, sayes the king, it is hot; looke how I sweat. No, sayes Jemy, the sunne blowes very colde. No, sayes the king, the winde shines very hot. The foole was almost angry to be crossed, and said hee would be hanged at night, if hee did sweat that day. With this merry talke they rode on; but one of the king's footmen hearing this, told the king at their return hee would make his grace laugh heartily. So the king very gallantly ranne that time, and neuer missed the glove, and so did the lords; which Jemy seeing, said it was nothing to doe. The king bade him runne; he did so, but the gloue lay still, and Jemy could not doe it. The king's footman (that matcht to doe him a good turne) said Jemy could doe it better blindfold. What, can he? quoth the king: I will neuer beleeue it. You shall see else, quoth hee; whereat Jemy maruelled much that without sight a man could doe that, which with all his might and sight he could not doe, was desirous to make tryall; so was blinded with a scarfe, while another tooke up the gloue, and was ready for the jest. Jemy runs: Now for my maisters, saies hee. They all shout aloud and cry rarely well done, and one unblindes him, while another puts the glove on the speare.

So simple hee was, that hee thought it was strange, and bragged all that day not a little. The king did alight, and went to drink wine at the Lord Hume's house, and Jemy went with him, while the footeman had time to worke his will, and mingling a conceit with butter (which I will not name, least some one should practise the like) clapt it under the saddle; and, as they rode to Edinborough, sayes the king, what say you to the weather now, Jemy? Mee thinks it is hotter than it was. Nay, it is colder, sayes he, for I begin to sweat.

The trotting of this mule made the mingled confection lather so, that it got into his breeches, and wroght up to the crowne of his head, and to the sole of his foote, and so he sweat profoundly. Still he whipt and he whipt, sweating more and more: they laught a good to see him in that taking. Now you must be hanged, says the king, as your bargaine was, for you sweat very much. What remedie? sayes hee. I am content to be hanged, but while I live after Ile never beleeue cold weather will make one sweat. No more will I, sayes the king, but hot weather will. Hot or colde, sayes Jemy, I am warme now, I am sure: I would I were ouer head and eares in some riuer to coole mee. So simple hee was that he knew not wether it was the sunne or the winde made him sweat. At night the king caused him to be washed and perfumed, yet he was scarce sweet twenty days after. Thus this fat foole chaft, but not in his owne grease.

Jemy, who was, as you have heard, a tall low man, and was swift of foote, on a time challenged the king's best footeman, for a wager, to run with him from the abbey, up the hill, to Cannegate (which stood entering to Edenborough, as Ludgate doth to London, and the King's place about Temple-barre.) The king being told of this challenge thought it would be good sport to see it performed, still perswaded Jemy to dare his footeman, who before denyed him, and knew fooles would talk any thing, though far unfit to perform any thing. Still the king would say he was made nimble to runne, and askt euery nobleman's judgement, who likewise soothed the king: it was so that they made him beleeue himself swift of foote, that I think in the end Jemy perswaded himselfe that none but fat men could run well, and nimble men, being light, would fall soonest; considering that light things, being of small substance, not feeling themselves, would surely fall. But here is the sport—the footeman, seeing it was the king's pleasure to see the wager tryed, dared him, which made Jemy mad, that he would run with him from Edinborough to Barwicke (which was forty miles) in one day; a thing as unpossible as to pull down a church in one houre, and to build it againe in another: for Jemy was lost in the king's company once of purpose, but fiue miles from the citty, at the Earle Morton's castle at da Keth, and they thought hee would neuer haue come home againe: when the king heard euery houre hee was comming, and still as hee entreated euery passenger to let him ride, by the king's watch in the high-way they had warning giuen to the contrary, for he was seauen days going the fiue myle: then, judge how long hee would be a running fortie. You will muse how hee did for meate all the time. Ile tell you how: he fasted all day, and went supperlesse to bed; but being in his first sound sleepe, meate was brought and laide by him, and a choppin of wine (for so they call it there) which made him at his coming to court tell the king that heauen was gentler than earthly men [who] would shew him no favour, neyther to ride nor feede him, when he was euery night cast into a sound sleepe; then when he wakt hee was sure of meate from heauen to feede on, when the meate came from the king's kitchen at Edenborough Abbey.

But to goe forward with our challenge. The king said the first word should stand, and on Jemie's head he laid a thousand marks: the Lady Carmichell, that laught to heare all this, wagered as much on the footeman's head. The day was appointed the next morning, being Thursday, to begin at fiue a'clock in the afternoone, in the coole of the euening, and eury one to his race must make him ready. Jemy, as he had seene the king's footeman doe, washt his feet with beere, and soakt them in butter; so all that night and the next day there was nothing but Jemy and his prouision to that great journey. The time came—Jemy was stript into his shirt, trust round for the purpose: the footeman and hee begins to runne; the footeman makes shew of great labour, and the foole made the substance, for he was quickly in a sweat. They puft and they blowede; they ran as swifte as a pudding would creepe. Jemy thought himselfe no smal foole to outrun the footeman, and did in his minde assure himselfe to win. The king laughs to see the toyle he made, and the footeman made great shew and little paines. By and by, Jemy calls for drinck; and the king, loath hee should haue any harme with labour, caused him to haue a mixed drincke to cast him into a sleepe; who, when he had drunck, as hee ran on his wager, he dropt downe in the streete, as heauy as if a leaden plummet, that makes a jack turne a spit, had fallen on the earth dab. There hee slept, and was carryed by commaund to the top of the hill, and laid downe againe: there hee slept halfe an houre, and when he wakt he remembered his journey. Seeing people still about him, up hee gets, away he jogs, and neuer lookes behinde him; and seeing Cannegate so neare him, had not the wit to wonder how hee came there, but laid hold on the ring of the gate, and staid to bee seene.

By and by the footeman comes sweating, with water poured on his face and head. O, my heart! sayes hee. O, my legs! sayes Jemy: I will not doe so much for all Scotland againe.

Well, Jemy cries Victory! victory! and there was the king's coach at hand to carry him home, for himselfe he neuer could haue gone, had his life lain on it. But when hee came home, the bragge hee made, the glory hee got, how hee outran the footman (and ran so easily as if he had been a sleepe) was wonderfull. I, it was sport enough for the king, a month after, to heare him tell it. Well, the king wonne the wager, he thought, and that was honour sufficient for him. Not three days after hee bad the king put away all his footemen, and hee would serue his turne to any place. The king thanked him for his good will, and said, when his neede was great, hee would make bold to use him. So Jemy, this fat foole, euer bragged of this wager.

There was a laundres of the towne, whose daughter used often to the court to bring home shirts and bands, which Jemy had long time loued and solicited, but to no end: she would not yeeld him an inch of her maidenhead. Now Jemy vowed he would haue it all: well, she consented at last; and, to be short, soone at night, at nine a'clocke, being in the winter, when shee knew her mother to bee gone to watch with a sick body, he should come, and all that night lye with her. Jemy, though witlesse, wanted no knavish meaning, thought long till it was night. But in the afternoone, this mayd goes up to the castle and gathers a great basket of nettles, and comming home strawes them under the bed. Night comes, nine a'clock strikes; Jemy on his horse comes riding forward, sets him up, and knockes at the doore: she lets him in, and bids him welcome, bonny man. To bed he goes; and Jemy euer used to lye naked, as is the use of a number, amongst which number she knew Jemy was one; who no sooner was in bed, but shee herself knocked at the doore, and herself askt who was there?—which, Jemy hearing, was afraid of her mother. Alas! sir (sayes shee), my mother comes, creepe under the bed. Jemy bustled not a little — under hee creepes, stark naked, where hee was stung with nettles. Judge, you that haue feeling of such matters: there hee lay, turning this way and that way; here hee stung his leg, there his shoulder, there his buttockes: but the mayde hauing lockt the doore to him, went to bed, and there lay he in durance (as they say) till morning. When the day broke, up gets the maide, to court she goes, and tels the king's chamberlaine of the matter, and hee told the king, who laughed thereat right heartily.

The chamberlaine was sent to see him there, who, when hee came, found him fast a sleepe under the bed, starke naked, bathing in nettles; whose skinne, when he wakened him, was all blistered grievously. The king's chamberlaine bid him arise and come to the king. I will not, quoth hee: I will go make my graue. See how things chanced! he shape truer than he was awar; for the chamberlaine going home without him tolde the king his answere. Jemy rose, made him ready, takes his horse and rides to the church-yard in the high towne, where he found the sexton (as the custom is there) making nine graues, three for men, three for women, and three for children; and whoso dyes next, first comes, first serued. Lend mee thy spade, sayes Jemy; and with that digs a hole, which hole hee bids him make for his graue, and doth giue him a French crowne. The man, willing to please him (more for his gold than his pleasure) did so; and the foole gets on his horse, and rides to a gentleman of the towne, and on the sodaine within two hours after dyed; of whom the sexton telling, hee was buried there indeed. Thus you see fooles haue a guess at wit sometime, and the wisest could haue done no more—not so much. But this fat foole fills a leane graue with his carkasse, upon which graue the king caused a stone of marble to bee put, on which the poets writ these lines in remembrance of him—

> He that gard all men till jeare,
> Jemy a Camber he ligges here;
> Pray for his sall, for he is geane,
> And here a ligges beneath this steane.

Is this possible, sayes the World, that I should bee so serued? Nay, thou art worse serued heareafter, sayes hee, for thou knowest not the following sceane; but attend it. By the foole is meant all fatnesse; by the king, Nature, that nurst him; by the nobles, such as sooth him; and by the ship, thee, in which many dangers are floating, through the sense of sinne:

and so, if life were awarranted fooles, fat ones, rich ones, would give the chaine of their soules, that is linked to saluaion, onely to inherit this earth in thy company; when earth, though it bee heauen to hell, by reason of the paines, yet the comparison auerts; it is hell to heauen in respect of pleasures.

By the second is meant the surfets of soule and body, that fooles buy with their gold, not sparing any price to please appetite, though the edge of it slice frome the bosome of good old Abraham very heauen itselfe.

By the third, how the fat fooles of this age will gronte and sweat under this massie burden, and purge to the crown from the foote, though their braine perish through the prevailing practise of busie endeauour. The mule, morrally signifies the diuell, upon whose trot their fatnesse takes ease, and rides a gallop to destruction.

By the fourth taile is prefigned the presumption of greatnesse, who are willing to outrun speede itselfe through greedy desire. In this is showne how flattery feedes them, placing before them, as in a sleepe, worke and wonder; when, to say sooth, all is not worth the wonder: their desire is more than abilitie to performe, and their practise above all; yet the nimble overshoot them in act, leauing them a quicknesse in will.

In the fifth, answere is made to the fourth, when often such forwarde deedes meete with backward lurches, and they are stung with their own follyes, netling very lust with shame and disgrace: it signifies adultery in fat ones, who (aboue their owne) whoring after strange gods, make their religion ride hackney to hell, and when shame takes them from the horse, they make their own graues, and are buried in their own shame, with this motto above written—

> Fat fooles gather to their woe
> Sorrow, shame, and care;
> Here they lye that gallopt so,
> In Deáth's ingraued snare.

This morrall motion gaue the World such a buffet, that she skrindge her face as though shee were pincht home; yet, seeing no remedy but that the flat and fat fooles should draw in her coach together, shee sets in the boote and rides on. The crittick reacheth his glasse to her view, and presents the third.

O! this was a humorous sir, indeede, leane Leonard: they call him a foole of strange and prepostrous breeding, begot of enuie, and out of doubt his base sonne: his description hath a straine of more wonder—long, like a lath, and of proportion little better; but giue his report hearing—

> Curled locks on idiots' heads,
>   Yeallow as the amber,
> Playes on thoughts as girls with beads,
>   When their masse they stamber.
> Thicke of hearing, yet thin ear'd,
>   Long of neck and visage,
> Hookie nosde and thicke of beard,
>   Sullen in his visage.
> Clutter fisted, long of arme,
>   Bodied straight and slender'd,
> Boisterous hipt, motley warme,
>   Euer went leane Leonard.
> Gouty leg'd, footed long,
>   Subtill in his follie,
> Shewing right, but apt to wrong,
>   When apeard most holy.
> Vnderstand him as he is,
>   For his marks you cannot misse.

You heare, maddam, sayes our cinnick, how he is markt: if ye meete him in your pottage-dish, yet know him. The World, though shee loued not the description, yet shee coucted his condition, and began to woe his report; which, making no bones of, the sweete youth gaue his doings thus.

In the merry forest of Shearewood dwells a kind gentleman, whose name I omit, fearing I too much offend in meddling with his foole; but I trust he will pardon me, for sithence, he is so well knowne thereabouts, I thinke it not amisse to tell it at London, that people seeing the strange workes of God, in his differing creatures, we that haue perfect resemblance of God, both in sence and similitude, may the better praise his name, that wee differ from them whose humours we read, see, and heare, are not so strange as true. I say againe this gentleman had a foole, Leonard they call[ed] him, leane of body, looking like enuie, whose conditions agree with his countenance. One time aboue all other, hee lockt himselfe into a parlour, where all alone hee played at slide groat, as his manner was: peices or counters he had none; yet, casting his hand empty from him, fly, saies hee : short with a vengeance ! then, play, saies hee (to his fellow) when, indeede, there is none but himselfe; but thus with supposes he playes alone, swaggers with his game fellow, out-sweares him with a thousand oaths, challenges him the field to answere him if hee bee a man, appoynts the place and all, that if any one not knowing his conditions should stand without and heare him, would thinke two swaggerers were fighting in the roome.

To his play againe he fals, seauen up for twelve pence, for that is his game still : well, they fall out, they go together by the eares, and such a hurly-burly is in the roome, that passes. At last the stooles they flye about, the pots they walke, the glasses they goe together; nay, the prayer-bookes they flie into the fire, that such a noise there was that the whole house wondered at his folly. Persuasions wer to no purpose; doores hee would open none, till they violently brake them open, though they were of gold; and so they did, and entered the parlour, found all this leuell coyle, and his pate broken, his face scratcht, and leg out of joynt; as a number say to this houre that hee is a play-fellow for the diuelle, and in game they cannot agree. But that is otherwise; for, in the great hall, at the seruing man's request, he will play by himselfe, if they will not play with him; and whoso playes with him, though they play for nothing, and with nothing, all is one, they must fall out; and if others be not by to part them, mischiefe may bee done, for he will lay it on, take it off who will : so that at his first comming he endaungered many, and now take heed is a faire thing, for few will come neere him. Thus you see that fooles that want wit to gouerne themselves well, have a wilfull will to goe forward in folly.

This leane, greedy foole having a stomacke, and seeing the butler out of the way, his appetite was such, as loath to tarry, breakes open the dairy house, eats and spoils new cheesecurds, cheesecakes, ouerthrowes creame bowles, and having filled his belly, and knew he had done euill, gets him gone to Mansfield in Sherwood, as one fearefull to be at home. The maydes came home that morning from milking, and finding such a masaker of their dairie, almost mad, thought a yeere's wages could not make amends. But, O the foole! leane Leonard, they cried, he did this mischief: they complayned to their master, but to no purpose; Leonard was farre enough off, search was made for the foole, but hee was gone, none knew wither; and it was his propertie, hauing done mischiefe, neuer to come home of himselfe, but if any one intreated him, he would easily be won. All this while the foole was at Mansfield in Sherwood, and stood gaping at a shoomaker's stall; who, not knowing him, asked him what he was? Goe looke, sayes hee: I know not myselfe. They asked him where hee was borne? At my mother's backe, sayes hee. In what country? quoth they. In the country, quoth hee, where God is a good man. At last one of these journeymen imagined he was not very wise, and flouted him very merrily, asking him if he would haue a stitch where there was a hole? (meaning his mouth). I, quoth the foole, if your nose may be the needle. The shoomaker could have found in his heart to have tooke measure on his pate with a last, instead of his foote, but let him goe as he was. A country plow-jogger being by, noting all this, secretly stole a peice of shoomaker's waxe off the stall, and coming behinde him, clapt him on the head, and asked him how he did? The foole, seeing the pitch ball, pulled to haue it off, but could not but with much paine, in an enuious spleene, smarting ripe runes after him, fals at fistie cuffes with him; but the fellow belaboured the foole cunningly, and got the foole's head under his arme, and bob'd his nose. The foole, remembring how his head was, strikes it up, and hits the fellowe's mouth with the pitcht place, so that the haire of his head and the haire of the clowne's beard were glued together. The fellow cryed, the foole exclaimed, and could not sodainely part: in the end, the people (after much laughing at the jest) let them part faire; the one went to picke his beard, the other his head. The constable came, askt the cause of their falling out, and knowing one to be Leonard, the leane foole, whom he had a warrant from the gentleman to search for, demands of the fellow how it hapned. The fellow hee could answere nothing, but um; um, quoth hee againe, meaning hee would tell him all when his mouth was cleane; but the constable thinking hee was mockt, clapt him in the stocks, where the fellow sat a long houre farming his mouth; and when hee had done, and might tell his griefe, the constable was gone to carry home Leonard to his maister, who, not at home, hee was enforced to stay supper-time, where hee told the gentleman the jest, who was very merrie to heare the story, contented the officer, and bad him set the fellow at liberty, who, betimes in the morning, was found fast asleepe in the stocks. The fellow knowing himselfe faulty, put up his wrongs, quickly departed, and went to work betimes that morning with a flea in his eare.

The gentleman with whom this Leonard dwelt, having bought a goodly fayre hawke, brought her home, being not a little proud of his penny-worth, and at supper to other gentlemen fell a praysing of her, who, soothing up his humour, likewise fayled not to adde a toarch of fire to encrease more flame; for indeede the bird was worthy of commendations, and therefore did merit prayses. Leonard standing by with his finger in his mouth, as it was his custome, after hearing them praise the goodnesse of the hawke, thought indeede they had meant for goodnesse, being farre better meate then a turkey or a swan, was very desirous to eate of the same; and unknowne goes downe, and sodainely from the pearch snatcht the hawke, and hauing wrung off her neck, begins to besiedge that good morsell, but with so good a courage, that the feathers had almost choakt him; but there lay my friend Leonard in a lamentable taking. Well, the hawke was mist, and the deede was found: the maister was fetcht, and all men might see the hawke, feathers and all, not very well digested. There was no boote to bid runne for drams to driue down this undigested moddicombe; the gentleman of the one side cryed, hang the foole! the foole on the other side cryed not, but made signes that his hawke was not so good as hee did praise her for; and, though the gentleman loued his hawke, yet he loued the foole aboue, being enforced rather to laugh at his simplicitie, then to vere at his losses sodainely—being glad to make himselfe merry, jested on it ever after. Upon whose hawke a gentleman of his very wisely writ these lynes, and gaue unto his maister.

Fooles feede without heede; unhappy be their feeding
Whose heed being in such speed, attempted without heeding;
May they choke that prouoke appetite by pleasure,
When they eate forbidden meate, and feede so out of measure.

The gentleman laughed at this rime, yet knew not whether more foole he for writing, the other for eating, or he for loosing. Well, putting the hare to the goose-giblets, seeing there was no remedy, made himselfe pastime, pleased himselfe, and did rest contented.

He that mischiefes many, sometime wrongs himselfe, as

hearken to this jest. Leonard of all things loued his wheelebarrow, and would worke all day, and carry dung in it, yet would sleepe in it at night — he would set up meate for his belly in it—I, what did hee without it. Once at a Christmas time, when the fire in the hall was full, Leonard was sore a cold: hee got coles out of the scullery, and put them into his barrow, and set them on fire, and so sate him downe to warme him, quite forgetting it was made of wood, and wood would burne: so, in the end, being warme, goes for a jacke of beere, brings it, and sets it on the fire to warme, so that the inside melted, and hee dranckt the drinck notwithstanding; but, on the sodaine, he seeing the wheele-barrow flame that he so loued, aloud hee cryes, Dmee! dmee! dmee! and takes it up flaming, and trundles it into the hall, among the people, to shew. The young men and maydes tumbled over one another for feare: some had their faces burned, others their leges; the maydes their smocks — yea, one set fire on another, for their aprons burned, and being many people, the flame increased rather then decreased. Leonard, seeing none would helpe him, runs (for feare lest the gentleman should know it) and thrusts it into the barne to hide it, which some seeing, runs after, and, had they not come at that time, the hay and straw had beene all burnt, for it was already of a light fire, but being quencht out all was well. Such is the enuie of fooles, who, seeing none would helpe him, thought to doe them mischiefe, which he did, but not much.

The World laughed a good at these jests, though, to say sooth, shee could hardly afford it, for feare of writhing her sweet fauour; yet strayning courtesy in this kinde, did, as our wantons doe at a feast, spare for manners in company, but alone cram most greedily. So shee, forgetting modesty, gapte out a laughter, and, like women hardly wonne, cryd More! more! The currish crittick said shee should, and gaue her the third pennerth of the morral, and said: You laugh at leane enuie in a long foole, but you have cause to weepe at long enuie in a leane age, as you liue in. This foole cries out not all mine, but distributes like a kinde companion, being a superficiall glasse to gaze in. There be leane fooles as well as fat: such are they whose noses dropes necessitie, and they smell out for church lands, many tenements, onthrifts, surfets, looking leanely on all this, but feede fatly on hope. This fatnesse goes to the heart, not seene in the visage. These seeme simple, but, like Leonard, hit home at advantage: they can stop men's mouths, and seale them up in advantage, and giue the stocks to the simple deseruer, when themselves are not blamlesse. O! beware when you see a long, meagre looke; search him—he hath also long, reaching fingers, and can slide a groat by himselfe, as Leonard did, fall out, curse, sweare, and batter heauen itselfe with humour of folly. Such was the leaneneckt crane, who had the fat foxe to dinner, making him lick the outside of the glasse, while his leannesse fed within. You understand me, maddame: such are your landlords to the poore, youre leane lords to the fat tennant, or by a figure one for the other. Thus they batten heere; but the diuell will gnaw their bones for it.

By the third jest we observe a greedinesse in leane folly, that, so good a report come in their way, these eat up hawke, feathers, and all, to put it by, though they choake in the deede. Hereupon comes in leane enuy, swallowes fat bits—I mean honest manners—and makes them sterril of all good manners, as the lawyer the poore clyant's plow pence, the cittie the country commodities; that, under the shew of leannesse, they fat themselves to the ribs—good hold for flesh hookes at the general waste. By the fourth and last (I would it were least) it bewrayes a curious and common leannesse in lewd liuers, who, to revenge on others, will fire their own wheelebarrow. Like the leane tennant, who, falling out with his landlord, and seeing his neighbour's house on fire, desired his neighbours to pull downe his first, for feare of more danger; not that he louede his neighbour's safety and his owne, but that hee hated his landlord : or the contrary, couetous of their owne commoditie, fire themselues, and, because they will not burn alone, endanger their friends, and say 'tis kind to have company. These are fooles, indeed, leane ones; these are fat and foule, and make thicke doings for the diuel's dyet. World, I name them not; thou knowest them well enough. At this shee bit her lip, knowing some that were leane Leonards in this; but kay me Ile kay thee : giue me an inch to day, Ile giue thee an ell to-morrow, and weele to hell together. The World, dimpling her chin with meere modestie, as it were throwing off variety of squemish nicetie, began to say, Sooth, thou saist true, there are such nicks in mee, but I know not how to mende : I am willing, but flesh is weake; prethee be more sparing, carpe not, confound not, hope the best amendment may come. Prethee goe in, furnish thy sallet: these hearbs already are sauory, and I picke out to my appetite, and though I bee not altogether pleased, yet am I not quite past patience : I will endure, for that disease that festers so much receives cure gladly, though it come with exceeding paine, yet so much the profit by how much the perplexities, cries cure to the danger. Mistris, sayes Sotto, I am glad to sit so neare you; and to bee thought a kinde neighbour, too, is more then the world affords. But looke, who is heere we have? we haue fellowde one with our flat, and fat foole disturbd by the leane. Now, as in a history we mingle mirth with matter, to make a please plaister for melancholy, so in our glasse we present to the leane a cleane. One that was more beloued among ladyes than thought can hatch, or opinion produce. His name is Jack Miller: he liues yet, and hath beene in this citie within few dayes, and giue me leaue to describe him thus —

> You that follie comprehend,
> Listen to my storie;
> This description well attend—
> I haue writ it for yee.

This cleane nigit was a foole,
Shapt in meane of all,
And of order fit to rule
Anger in her loudest brawl.
Fat and thicke, neate and cleane,
And delights in pleasure,
Saue a nasty ugly straine
Of an other measure
From his nostrils rumatick.
Griefe it was to see
Such a simple neatnesse spring
From imbisillitie.
Creatures of the better sort,
For the foole was cleane,
Gaue him loue with good report,
Had not this ill beene.
But let slip it was no fault,
Men as slougish be,
Since the wisest jump as short
In all cleanlynesse as he.

Alas! quoth the World, I am sorry, trust me, that one so outwardly well should bee so inwardly ill, and haue that appearance in nastie defect, which of itselfe is neate; but go on with the repetition, since wee are mended in the condition. Wee will winck at small faults, tho wee yeelde it greate in nature. Nemo sine crimine, and so forth. I, quoth Sotto, say yee me so? haue at him then, out it goes, but mark it well.

In a gentleman's house where Jack Miller resorted, as he was welcome to all, it chanced so there was a play, the players dressed them in the gentleman's kitchen, and so entered through the entry into the hall. It was after dinner, when pyes stood in the oven to coole for supper: Jack had not dyned, and seeing the oven stand open, and so many pyes there untold, (hee thought because they seemed numberlesse) O! sayes

Jack, for one of them p— p— pyes, for so hee stammered in speaking. The players boy being by, and in his ladyes gowne, could haue found in his heart to creepe in, cloathes and all; but he perswaded Jack to do so, to which hee was willing, and very nimbly thrusts his head into the hot oven, which being newly opened, on the sodaine hee was singed both of head and face, and almost not a hayre left on his eye-brows or beard. Jack cryes, O! I burne, and had not the wit to come back, but lay still: the gentlewoman-boy tooke him by the heeles, and pulled him out, but how he lookt I pray you judge that can discerne fauours. Jack was in a bad taking with his face, poore soule, and lookt so ugly and so strangely, that the lady of the play, being ready to enter before the gentiles to play her part, no sooner began, but, remembring Jack, laught out, and could goe no further. The gentleman mused at what hee laught, but such a jest being easily seene, was told the gentleman, who sent in for Jack Miller, who came like bald Time, to tell them time was past of his hayre: but hee so strangely lookt, as his countenance was better then the play. But against night the players dress themselves in another place; and at supper Jack Miller sang his song of Dirryes Faire, with a barmy face to take out the fire, and lookt like the poter of the ale-fat. It was no boote to bid him stut and stammer, poore foole: as cleane as he was, hee was now but beastly faced, for hee looked like a man that, being ashamed to shew his face, had hid it in a dry lome wall, and pulling it out againe left all the hayre behinde him.

Jack, on Newyeeres day in the morning, was to carry a Newyeeres gift to a gentleman a myle off, and as he staid to have it delivered him to beare, asked which was the cleanest way thither. A fellow, knowing his cleanlinesse, sends him over a durty marsh; and so hee folded up his band (then cleane) for fouling, that at the gentleman's doore he might put it on. The present came, which Jack seeing, made legs to the gentlewoman, forgetting his band was in his hose, carried a stif neck to and fro to the gentlewoman, and what ere she spake, or where shee stood, Jack would look but one way, as though his neck had been starcht. And, remember, saies the gentlewoman, you abuse not my message, nor my gift: No, fo, fo, forsooth, sayes Jack; and away he goes, and thought hee would see what it was, and, as hee went he lift up the basket lid and lookt. Ah, ha! quoth Jack, I see it is almond bu—, bu—, butter.

Along he goes, and seeing the marsh wet and durty, thought to leape a little ditch, and so to goe a cleane hie way, but (O! poor Jack) hee, basket and all, lay in the midst of the ditch up to his arme-pits in mud; which, Jack seeing, got out, and goes to a riuer by, and washes himselfe first, his band next; where, if it had been about his neck as it should, it had labour well saued: but he washt his almond butter so long, that the butter was washt away, which hee perceiuing, in that woefull taking comes back, and called for more bu—, bu—, butter. The gentlewoman seeing how things went, rather laught then vext, because shee was so simple to trust a foole with matters of trust, and bad him get him to the fire and dry him; and said next time she would stay her seruants leisure, (who then were abroad) rather then trust to a rotten staffe. Thus cleane fooles light still on beastly bargaines.

In the towne of Esam, in Worstersh., Jack Miller being there borne, was made much of in every place. It hapned that the Lord Shandoye's players came to towne and played there; which Jack not a little loved, especially the clowne, whom he would embrace with a joyful spirit, and call him Grumball, for so he called himselfe in gentleman's houses, where hee would imitate playes, being all himselfe king, gentleman, clowne, and all: hauing spoke for one, he would sodainely goe in, and againe return for the other; and, stammering as he did, make much mirth: to conclude, he was a right innocent, without any villany at all.

When these players I speake of had done in the towne, they went to Partiar, and Jack said he would goe all the world over with Grumbal. It was then a great frost new begun, and the hauen was frozen over thinely; but heere is the wonder, the gentleman that kept the Hart, (an inne in the towne) whose backside looked to the way that led to the riuer-side to Partiar, lockt up Jack in a chamber next the hauen, where he might see the players passe by; and they of the towne, loth to lose his company, desirued to have it so; but hee, I say, seeing them goe by, creepes through the window, and said, I come to thee, Grumball. The players stood all still to see further. He got down very dangerously, and makes no more adoe, but venters over the hauen, which is by the long bridge, and, as I guess, some forty yards ouer; yet he made nothing of it, but my hart aked when my eares heard the ise crack all the way. When hee was come unto me I was amazed, and tooke up a brick-bat (which lay there by) and threw it, which no sooner fell on the ise, but it burst. Was not this strange, that a foole of thirty yeares was borne of that ise which would not endure the fall of a brick-bat? but euery one rated him for the deede, telling him of the daunger. He considered his fault, and, knowing faults should be punished, he intreated Grumball the clowne, who hee so deerely loued, to whip him but with rosemary, for that he thought would not smart. But the players in jest breecht him till the bloud came, which he tooke laughing, for it was his manner euer to weepe in kindnesse, and laugh in extreames. That this is true mine eies were witnesses, being then by.

Jack Miller, welcomed to all places, and bard of none, came to a gentleman, who being at dinner requested him for mirth to make him a play, which he did, and to sing Derries Faire, which was in this manner. First it is to be notted, hee strutted hugely, and could neyther pronounce b nor p., and thus he began.

As I went to Derries Faire, there was I ware of a jolly begger,
Mistris Annis M. Thomas, under a tree mending of shoone,
Mistris Annis M. Thomas, night braue beggars euery one.

And so forward; but the jest was to heare him pronounce braue beggars, and his qualitie was, after hee began his song, no laughing could put him out of it. One standing by, noting his humour that b and p plagued him, bad him say this after him, which Jack said he would doe: Buy any flawre, pasties, pudding pyes, plum pottage, or pes-cods. O! it was death to Jack to doe it; but like a willing foole he fell to it. Buy any, buy any fla—, flaw—, p—, p—, p—, pasties, and p—, p—, p—, pudding, p—, p—, p—, pyes, p—, p—, p—, &c. And euer as hee hit the on word, hee would pat with his finger on the other hand, that more and more it would make a man burst with laughing almost to see his action: sometime he would be pronouncing one word, while one might goe to the doore and come againe. But euer after gentiles would request him to speake that, where before, Derryes fayre was all his song.

He came not long after (to this I am witness, because my eares heard it) to a gentleman's not far from Upton upon Seuerne, in Gloxester-shire, where at the table among many gallants and gentlewomen, (almost the state of the country) hee was to jest and sing: especially they intreated him for his new speech of the pees, which he began in such manner to speake with driuelling and stuttering, that they began mightely to laugh; insomuch, that one proper gentlewomen among the rest, because shee would not seeme too immodest with laughing, for such is the humour of many, that thinke to make all, when God knows they marre all: so she, straining herself, though inwardly she laughed heartily, gave out such an earnest of her modesty, that all the table rung of it. Who is that? says one: not I, says another; but by her cheeks you might find guilty Gilbert, where he had hid the brush. This jest made them laugh more, and the rayther that shee stood upon her marriage, and disdained all the gallants there, who so heartily laught, that an old gentlewoman at the table took such a conceit at it with laughing, that, had not the foole bin which stood (by fortune) at her back, and was her supporter, being in a great swound, she had fallen to the ground backward. But downe they burst the windows for ayre, and there was no little boot to bid ront : shee was nine or ten dayes ere she recovered that fit on my knowledge. Thus simple Jack made mirth to all, made the wisest laugh, but to this gathered little wit to himselfe.

This, quoth the World, is mere mirth without mischiefe, and I allow of it : folly without faults, is as reddish without salt, may passe in digestion one without the other, and doe better, where both together engenders but rheume, and mirth does well in any. I, says Sotto, so way you not the true waight : as it is sufferable to be whole, so it is saluable to be hurt, and one to the other giues ayme ; but [to] bee neither is monstrous. I would faine morrall of it, if you please. Leave was granted, for the World knew it would else be commanded, and Sotto thus poynts at the parable.

By the first merry emblem I reach at stars, how they fire themselves in the firmament : whether it bee sitting to neere the sunne in the day, or couching to neere the moone in the night, I know not ; but the hayre of their happynesse often fals off, and shoots from a blazing commet to a falne star, and carries no more light then is to be seene in the bottome of Platoe's inck-horne ; and, where they should study in private with Diogenes in his cell, they are with Cornelius in his tub.

By the second, the cleane fooles of this world are pattern'd, who so neately stand upon their ruffes, and shoeties, that the braine is now lodged in the foote ; and thereupon comes it that many make their head their foote, and employment is the drudge to prodigalitee, made sawcie through the mud of their owne minds, where they so often stick fast, that Bankes, his horse, with all his strength and cunning, cannot draw them out.

By the third is figured saucie adventure in folly ; for wisdome puts no forward[er] then warrant, and for pleasure the wisest make themselves fooles.

To conclude this foolish description of the fourth, many sing out their tunes, and like ideots true borne, confound with folly what was created more holy, shutting out trifles that out method matter of more waight, where nisetie herselfe will let goe in laughter, though she spoyle her marriage.

The World likte not this well, but bit the lip againe, but as rich men suffer wrongs for advantage, took her pennerth's together, casts her eye aside, and sees a comely foole indeed passing more stately, and, who was this? forsooth, Wil. Sommers, one not meanly esteemed by the king for his merriment: his mellody was of a higher straine, and he lookt as the noone broade waking. His description was writ in his fore-head, and yee might read it thus :—

> Will. Sommers born in Shropshire, as some say,
> Was brought to Greenwich on a holy day,
> Presented to the king; which foole disdain'd
> To shake him by the hand, or else asham'd:
> How er'e it was, as ancient people say,
> With much adoe was wonne to it that day.
> Leane he was, hollow eyde, as all report,
> And stoop he did, too; yet in all the court
> Few men were more belou'd then was this foole,
> Whose merry prate kept with the king much rule.
> When he was sad, the king and he would rime:
> Thus Will exiled sadness many a time.
> I could describe him as I did the rest,
> But in my mind I doe not think it best:
> My reason this; how ere I doe descry him,
> So many knew him that I may belye him;
> Therefore, to please all people, one by one,
> I hold it best to let that paines alone:
> Onely this much,—hee was a poor mans friend,
> And helpt the widdow often in the end.
> The king would euer grant what he would craue,
> For well he knew Will no exacting knave:

But whisht the king to doe good deeds great store,
Which caus'd the court to loue him more and more.

The World was in loue with this merry foole, and said he was fit to the time indeede, and therefore deserued to be well regarded. Insomuch as shee longed to heare his friscoes morralized, and his gambals set downe. And Sotto as willingly goes forward thus.

Will Sommers, in no little credit in the king's court, walking in the parke at Greenwich, fell asleepe on the stile that leads into the walk, and many that would haue gone that way so much loued him, that they were loth to disease him, but went another way; I, the better sort, for now adaies beggars are gallants, while gentiles of right blood seeme tame ruffians; but note the loue Will Sommers got. A poore woman, seeing him sleepe so dangerously, eyther to fal backward, or to hurt his head leaning so against a post, fetcht him a cushion and a rope; the one for his head, and the other to bind him to the post, from falling backward: and thus hee slept, and the woman stood by, attending as the groom of his chamber. It chanced so, that upon great occasion, as you shall after heare, Will Sommers uncle came out of Shropshire to seeke him in the court; a plaine old man of threescore yeeres, with a buttoned cap, a lockram falling band, course but cleane, a russet coat, a white belt of a horse hide, right horse-coller white leather, a close, round breech of russet sheeps wool, with a long stock of white kersey, a high shoe with yelow buckles, all white with dust; for that day the good old man had come three and twenty miles on foot. This kinde old man, comming up in his countrys behalfe, and comming into Greenwitch, asked the way to the court: euery one directs him; but one villaine page directs him by the court gate, to crosse in a boat over to Blackwal, and told him that was the court. The silly old man willingly paid his penny before hand, and was going ouer; but some that ouer-heard their talk, hindered his journey and laughed at the jest, yet pitied his simplicitie, and sets him in the right way. When he came in and saw such a place, he was amazed, and stood gazing, which the gard and gentlewomen, in their windows, had much sport to see. At last one asked him what he was? The old man answeres, A poore Shropshire man; and demands if there were not a gentleman in the court dwelling, called by the name of M. Will Sommers? for the country hearing him in fauour in the court, said hee was so at least. The courtier answered, Here is such a one indeede. For fault of a worse, saies hee, I am his uncle; and wept with joy that hee should see him. Marry, says the man, Ile help you to him straight; for, I tell you, not any in the court durst but haue sought him, which this man did, and it was told him. Hee was walkt into the parke, while the king slept that hote day. Thether went they to seeke him. All this while my friend Will was in counsel with the post; and the cushion stood as arbitrator betwixte them, and the woman as a witnesse what was said and done. At last came these two and wakened him. William, seeing his head soft, What soft post is this? quoth he. A post of mine own making, saies the woman. But she lost nothing by her good will; for ere she left Wil Sommers, shee got him to get her sons pardon of the king, who was to bee hanged three days after for piracy: but by Will Sommers means he deceived the hang-man. This and many good deedes he did to diuers.

The foole, being wakened, lookes about him; when he had thanked the woman, asked what newes? sayes the man, Sir, here is your uncle come out of the country to see you. God a mercy cousin! sayes Will Sommers; I thank thee for thy labour, you cannot uncle me so. Yes, truly, sir, I am your own deare uncle, M. William, and with that wept. Are you my uncle? sayes Will. I, sir, sayes hee. Are you my uncle? sayes hee againe. I, sure, and verely too. But are you my uncle, indeed? By my vusse I am, sayes the old man. Then, uncle, by my vusse, welcome to court, sayes Will Sommers. But what make you heere, uncle? He ups and tels his comming to him. Will takes him by the hand: Come, saies hee, thou shalt see Harry, onckle — the onely Harry in England; so he led him to the chamber of presence, and euer and anon cryes out, Aware, roome for me and my uncle! and knaues bid him welcome. You are welcome, sir, said they: the old man thought himselfe no earthly man, they honoured him so much.

But Will, ready to enter the presence, lookes on his uncle, and seeing him not fine enough to looke on the king: Come, uncle, sayes hee, we will haue your geere mended; leads him to his chamber, and attires him in his best fooles coate, simply, God wot, meaning well to him; and the simple old man as simply put it on, cap and all.

But they come; and up they came, and to the king they goe, who, being with the lord treasurer alone, merry, seeing them two, how Will had got another foole, knew there was sport at hand. How now! sayes the king, What news with you? O, Harry! sayes he, this is my owne uncle; bid him welcome. Wel, said the king, he is welcome. Harry, sayes hee, heare me tell thee a tale, and I will make thee rich, and my uncle shall be made rich by thee. Will tels the king how Terrils Frith was inclosed. Tirrels Frith! sayes the king; what is that? Why, the heath where I was borne, called by the name of Tirrels Frith: now a gentleman of that name takes it all in, and makes people beleeue it is all his, for it took the name from him; so that, Harry, the poore pine, and their cattle are all undone without thy help. And what should I doe? sayes the king. Marry, sayes Will, send to the Bishop of Hereford; hee is a great man with Terril: commaund him to set the Frith at liberty againe, who is now imprisoned by his means. And how shall I be rich by that? sayes the king. The poore will pray for thee, sayes Will; and thou shalt bee rich in heauen, for on earth thou art rich already. All this was done, and Wills uncle went home, who, while he liued, for that deed was allowed bayly of the common, which place was worth twenty pound a yeere.

Howseuer, these three things it came in memory, and are for mirth incerted into stage playes I know not, but that Will Sommers asked them of the king, it is certaine : there are some will affirme it now living at Greenwich. The king being on a time extreame melancholy, and full of passion, all that Will could doe will not make him merry. Ah! sayes hee, this must haue, must haue a good showre to clense it; and with that goes behinde the arras. Harry, saies hee, Ile goe behind the arras, and study three questions, and come againe ; see, therefore, you lay aside this melancholy muse, and study to answere me. I, quoth the king : they will be wise ones, no doubt. At last out comes William with his wit, as the foole of the play does, with an anticke looke to please the beholders. Harry, sayes hee, what is it, that the lesser it is, the more it is to be feared? The king mused at it; but, to grace the jest better, he answered, he knew not. Will answered, it was a little bridge ouer a deepe riuer ; at which hee smyled.

What is the next, William ? sayes the king. Marry, this is the next : what is the cleanliest trade in the world ? Marry, sayes the king, I think a comfit-maker, for hee deales with nothing but pure ware, and is attired cleane in white linen when hee sels it. No, Harry, sayes [he to] the king ; you are wide. What say you, then ? quoth the king. Marry, sayes Will, I say a durt-dauber. Out on it, says the king, that is the foulest, for hee is durty up to the elbows. I, sayes Will; but then he washes him cleane againe, and eats his meate cleanly enough. I promise thee, Will, saies the king, thou hast a pretty foolish wit. I, Harry, saies he, it will serue to make a wiser man than you a foole, methinks. At this the king laught, and demaunds the third question. Now, tell me, saies Will, if you can, what it is that, being borne without life, head, lippe, or eye, yet doth runne roaring through the world till it dye. This is a wonder, quoth the king, and no question ; I know it not. Why, quoth Will, it is a fart. At this the king laught hartely, and was exceeding merry, and bids Will aske any reasinable thing, and he would graunt it. Thanks, Harry, saies he; now against I want, I know where to find it, for yet I neede nothing, but one day I shall, for euery man sees his latter end, but knows not his beginning. The king understoode his meaning, and so pleasantly departed for that season, and Will laid him downe among the spaniels to sleepe.

Of a time appointed the king dined at Windsor, in the chappel yard at Cardinall Wolsey's, at the same time when he was building that admirable worke of his tombe: at whose gate stoode a number of poore people, to be serued with alms when dinner was done within; and, as Will passed by, they saluted him, taking him for a worthy personage, which pleased him.

In he comes, and finding the king at dinner, and the cardinall by attending, to disgrace him that he neuer loued, Harry, says hee, lend me ten pound. What to doe? saies the king. To pay three or foure of the cardinall's creditors, quoth hee, to whom my word is past, and they are come now for the money. That thou shalt, Will, quoth hee. Creditors of mine? saies the cardinall: Ile give your grace my head if any man can justly aske me a penny. No! saies Will. Lend me ten pounds; if I pay it not where thou owest it, Ile give thee twenty for it. Doe so, saies the king. That I will, my liege, saies the cardinall, though I know I owe none. With that he lends Will ten pounds. Will goes to the gate, distributes it to the poore, and brought the empty bag. There is thy bag againe, saies hee: thy creditors are satisfied, and my word out of danger.

Who received? sayes the king; the brewer or the baker? Neyther (Harry), saies Will Sommers. But, cardinall, answere me in one thing: to whom dost thou owe thy soule? To God, quoth hee. To whom thy wealth? To the poore, sayes hee. Take thy forfeit (Harry) sayes the foole; open confession, open penance: his head is thine, for to the poore at the gate I paid his debt, which hee yeelds is due: or if thy stony heart will not yeeld it so, saue thy head by denying thy word, and lend it mee: thou knowest I am poore, and haue neyther wealth nor wit, and what thou lendest to the poore God will pay thee ten fold; he is my surety—arrest him—for, by my troth, hang mee when I pay thee. The king laught at the jest, and so did the cardinall for a shew, but it grieved him to jest away ten pound so: yet worse tricks then this Will Sommers serued him after, for indeede hee could neuer abide him, and the forfeiture of his head had liked to haue beene payed, had hee not poysoned himselfe.

There was in the time of Will Sommers another artificiall foole, or jester, in the court, whose subtiltie heapt up wealth by gifts giuen him, for which Will Sommers could neuer abide him; but, indeede, lightly one foole cannot indure the sight of another, as Jack Oates, the minstrell, in the fat foole's story, and one beggar is woe that another by the doore should goe. This jester was a big man, of a great voyce, long black locks, and a verry big, round beard. On a time, of purpose, Will Sommers watcht to disgrace him, when he was jugling and jesting before the king. Will Sommers brings up a messe of milke and a manchet: Harry, saies hee, lend me a spoone. Foole, saies the jester, use thy hands, helpe hands, for I haue no lands, and meant, that saying would warrant his grose feeding. I, saies Will Sommers, beasts will doe so, and beasts will bid others doe as they doe themselves. Will, said the king, thou knowest I haue none. True Harry, saies hee, I know that, therefore I askt thee; and I would (but for doing thee harme) thou hadst no tongue to grant that foole his next sute; but I must eate my creame some way. The king, the jester, and all gathers about him to see him eate it. Will begins thus to rime ouer his milk:

This bit, Harry, I giue to thee, and this next bit must serue for mee, both which Ile eate apace;
This, madame, unto you, and this bit I myself eate now, and all the rest upon thy face.

Meaning the foole, in whose beard and head the bread and
milk was thicke sowne, and his eyes almost put out. Will
Sommers hee gets him gone for feare. This lusty jester, forgetting himself, in fury draws his dagger, and begings to pro-
test. Nay; saies the king, are ye so hote? claps him fast, and,
though hee draws his dagger here, makes him put it up in another place. The poore abused jester was jested out of countenance, and lay in durance a great while, till Will Sommers
was faine, after he broke his head, to giue him a plaister, to
get him out againe. But neuer after came my jugler in the
court more so neere the king, being such a dangerous man to
draw in the presence of the king.

Now, Lady World, saies Sotto, you wonder at this first
jest: do not; 'tis common, for who so simple that, being gorged
with broth themselues, will not giue their friends one spoonful,
especially our kinne. O weell to make them great, make our-
selues, and pollitikly rise againe by their greatness. But hee
was simple in that; for though hee raised many, hee himselfe
stood at one stay. But the deed is not common, therefore may
fitly be termed a fooles deed, since the wise meddle not with
it, unlesse to plunge further in, and winde from povertie. But
leaue it the greatest power of all to remedie and reuenge,
while earthly majestie grows great by adding libertie to their
afflictions, as in our commons of late, God preserue him for it.

By the second morally signification giues this; that fooles
questions reach to mirth, leading wisdome by the hand, as age
leads children by one finger, and though it holds not fast in
wisdome, yet it points at it.

Better so then the wise to put questions to fooles; for that's
to put money out of the bag, and leaue the money behinde to
bad use, while themselues beg with the bag. Such, like Will
Sommers, sleepe amongst dogs. The third bids us charitably
learne of simplicitie to pay our debts when the poore creditor
cals for it; but 'tis a generall fault, and such who haue doores
shut, whereat the poore stand, shal find gates fast whereat

themselues may not enter; but especially we of the laity, for while the pastor cherishes the soule, we seeke to starve the body; but let's be mindfull least decaying one we lose both.

O! the World could not indure this, but offered to fling away. Nay, nay, saies the cinnick; soft and faire — a word or too more: and, halfe angry, looking into his glasse, sees one all in blew, carrying his neck on the one side, looking sharply, drawing the leg after him in a strange manner, described in meeter thus:

> Some thing tall, dribling euer,
> Bodie small, merrie neuer,
> Splay footed, visage black,
> Little beard, it was his lack,
> Flat capt still in view,
> The citties charge many knew;
> Long coated, at his side
> Muckinder and inckhorne tied,
> Preaching still unto boyes,
> Ayming well, but reaching toyes:
> Louing all, hating none,
> Lesse such as let him not alone;
> As a liude, so a dyde;
> Was death's scorne, though life's pride.

This is singular, indeede, sayes the World: I long to heere of this dry, poore John. His name is John, indeede, saies the cinnick; but neither John a nods, nor John a dreames, yet either as you take it, for he is simply simple without tricks, not sophisticated like your tobacco to tast strong, but as nature aloud him he had his talent. Whereat the World so tickled her spleene that she was agog, clap[ped] her hands for joy, and saies she was deeply satisfied, and cryed more. The crooked stick of liqurish that gaue this sweet relish, being to set his teeth to it, wipes his rheumy beard, and smites his philosophical nose,

E

snapping his fingers, barber-like after a dry shauing, jogs on thus:

This innocent ideot, that neuer harmed any, before I enter tany furher, I will let you understand in too words, how he came to be of the hospital of Christschurch.

Some certaine yeers since (but not a few yeers) there dwelt a poore blinde woman in Bow-lane, in London, called by the name of blinde Alice, who had this foole of a child to lead her; in whose house he would sit eyther on the stayres, or in a corner, and sing psalms, or preach to himselfe of Peter and Paul, because he delighted to goe to sermons with blinde Alice, and heard the preacher talk of them. It chanced the Worshipfull of the Citty (good benefactours to the poore) to take her into Christ's hospital, with whom John went as a guide to lead her: who being old, after shee dyed, hee was to bee turned out of doore; but the Citty, more desirous to pitty then to be cruell, placed him as a fostred fatherless child, and they did wel in it too, seeing hee was one of God's creatures, though some difference in persons. Well, to goe forward in what I promised you: John went to St. Paul's church, in London, to meet with B. Nowell, the deane, whose bounty to him was great; and the foole knew it well enough, whom he would duly attend after his preaching, for euer at their meeting he gaue them a groat, and hee would bring it to his nurse. Well, B. Deane preached not that day; whereupon John stands in a corner, with boyes flocking about him, and begins to preach himselfe, holding up his muckender for his booke, and reads his text. It is written, saies he, in the 3 chapter of Paule to the Corinthians. Brethren, you must not sweare (for that was lightly all his text): then thus he begins.—Wheras or wherunto it is written; for because you must belieue it; for surely else we are no Christians. Write the sermon (boy) saies hee (as the hospital boyes doe) and then one must write on his hand with his finger, and then he would goe forward thus. The world is proud, and God is angry if wee do not repent.

Good friend giue me a pin, or good friend giue me a poynt, as it came in his minde. And so sucking up his driuell and his breath together, would pray and make an end: which being done, who bids me home to dinner, now? saies John. The boyes that knew his qualities, answeres that do I, John. Thank ye, friend, saies he, and goes home to his own dwelling at Christ's Church. But, at this time, one wealthy merchant's son, to make his father merry, bad him home to dinner indeede, and, will hee or nill hee, he must goe with him. With much adoe, John went; and, coming into the house, simply sits him downe, as his use was, in the chimney corner. It was in Lent, when pease pottage bare great sway, and when euery pease must have his ease. John, beholding pease pottage on the fire, thought on his nurse, for he was all sauing for her, and seeing nobody by, stept to the pot, and put a great ladle of pottage into his pocket, and pittiously burnt his thigh; and but that the leather was thick, it had beene worse. John, feeling something burne, lept and cryed: they ran in to see the matter why he cryed, but more and more he exclaimed, I burn! I burn! and got out of doores, and neuer leaues it, til he came to his nurse, who quickly shifted him, and mended what was amisse. But the jest was to see the folk of the house, who, wondering what he ayled, could not deuise what the matter was; but a begger in the entry, who beheld all, told the truth of the matter, who lost a good alms for his labour. But thus simple John, by his own folly, died the inside of his pocket pease pottage tawny, and set a good scarlet red upon his thigh.

Gaffer Homes, being sexton of Christ's Church, would often set John aworke to toull the bell to prayers or burials, wherin he delighted much: it chanced so, that comming through the church, and hauing nothing to doe, seeing the bell so easily to be come by, towles it. The people, as the custom is, repairs to church (as they used) to know for whom it was. John answeres them still, for his nurse's chicken. They said, wherefore towles the bell, John? I know not. When dyed he?

Even now. Who, John? Who, my nurse's chicken, quoth hee, and laughs. This jest was knowne to euery neighbour thereabouts, who sent him to bid him leaue touling; but it was not his custome, till Goodman Homes tooke the rope from him that gaue the rope to him. Well, there stood Jack, towling, from foure a'clock to sixe, goodman Homes being from home, who was not a little vext at John's dilligence, but laid the rope euer after where John could not reach it. John was of this humor: ask him what his coat cost him? he would say a groat; what his cap, band, or shirt cost? all was a groat; aske what his beard cost? and still a groat. So, one Friday morning there was a gentleman to ride down into Warwickshire, about payment of an hundred pound upon a bond's forfeiture: the time was next day, by sunset; it was no boote to bid him pull on his boots and be gone. Well, he made hast and went to doe it without bidding; and yet, for all his haste, his bootes were seeme-rent, and must haue a stitch or two needes: he sends them to a cobler, next to Christ's Church gate in Newgate market, who was diligent to mend them straight; and as he had done, comes John of the hospitall to him (as his use was) to carry home his work, and he sends John home with the boots. As John was going through Iuy lane, a country fellow that knew him not, meets him, and seeing the boots, What shall I giue thee for them? saies hee. John (who sold euery thing for a groat) asked a groat. The fellow, seeing it was a good penniworth, giues him a groat and departs with the boots. John, as his use was, gaue it to his nurse. She asked him where hee had it? Hee said for boots; but she not knowing his minde, fell to worke againe as he found her.

The forfeiture of the bond so hammered in this gentleman's head, that he thought euery houre two, till he had his boots, and mused they came not from mending, sends for them presently. One comes sweating (zoones!) cobler, the boots: and being at worke very busie, I, sayes hee, they are mended and carryed home. Another comes, boots! boots!

Would the boots were in your belly, quoth the cobler; once againe, they are gone home. By and by comes the gentleman in his white linen boot hose, ready to the purpose. A poxe of lazy coblers! sayes hee; my boots! shall I forfeit a bond for your pleasure? The cobler puts off his considering cap. Why, sir, sayes hee, I sent them home but now. By whom? sayes he. By John, blew John, sayes the cobler. The gentleman he runs home one way, the cobler another. Well, no boots were to be had. The gentleman hee stayed, and the cobler hee prayed, but all this while the boots belaid and came not. The cobler seekes John at his nurse's, where he was, and found the boots were sold for a groat. The cobler seeing no remedy, because the gentleman was in haste, giues him fiue shillings, with a heauy hey ho, towards a new paire, and lost foure shillings, eight pence, by the bargaine; but the cobler would neuer let John carry home his ware more. Nay, sayes the cobler, if my money can be booted and ride poste so by fiue shillings at a time, it is no boot for me to say utinm, but the next bootes Ile make a page of my own age, and carry home myselfe, for I see fooles will afford good penniworths.

On Easter Sunday the ancient custome is that all the children of the hospitall goe before my Lord Maior to the Spittle, that the world may witnesse the works of God and man, in maintennance of so many poore people, the better to stir up liuing men's minds to the same good. Before which the children of the hospitall, like a captaine, goes John; whom, to behold the people flock apace, and the weather being hot, their thrusting made John extreme dry. John considered he was like to fast while dinner, yet kept on his rank to the spittle, where the cannes did walke apace by his nose, but neuer came at him, which made him more eager of drinck. Well, while the children were placing, John stood making of water, and seeing a gentleman's doore open, slips in, and the houshold without, standing to see my Lord Maior passe by, regarded him [not]; but hee whose nose had wit to smell good beere, got downe into

the seller, and fell to it tipple square, till he was lost and quite
drunck, and lay'd himselfe to sleepe behinde two barrels, and
unseene slept all that day. In the sermon time he was mist,
sought, and not found. The afternoone came ; the gentleman's
butler and other good fellowes fell to carouse soundly, till the
butler was layd up too : heere was a seller well fraught with
fooles; but all this while the beadles fayled not to search up
and downe the citie : the cryer cryed a man child, of the age
of two and thirtie yeeres, for at least hee was so old. But
returne we to the seller. The two drunkards waked both together. John cals nurse! nurse! which the butler (halfe awake)
hearing, thought the diuell had bin playing bo peep with him ;
but when he looked and beheld him, imagining how it was, he
secretly sent him to the hospitall, least hee were blamed for his
negligence in looking to the doore no better.

A number of things more John did, which I omit, fearing to
be tedious. Not long after he dyed, and was old — for his
beard was full of white haires, as his picture in Christ's Hospital (now to be seene) can witnesse : buryed he is, but with
no epitaph. Mee thinks, those that in his life time could afford
him his picture, might with his graue yeeld him so much as
foure lynes, that people may see where he lyes, whom they so
well knew : and if I might persuade, his motto should be to
this effect :

> Here sleeps blew John, that giues
> Food to feede wormes, and yet not liues.
> You that passe by, looke on his graue,
> And say yourselues the like must haue.
> Wise men and fooles all one end makes :
> Gods will be done, who giues and takes.

Surely, says Mistress Nicetie, this pleases well to see one
so naturally silly to be simply subtill : it is strange; but I
heare it, and, like a tale out of a poore man's mouth, hardly
credit it.

This foole, says Sotto, signifies many who come to church to meete acquaintance, more than for piety, and will sooner sell the church for mony, then pawne ought to underprop it. At these the boyes and children of this world wonder, while manly age sees and will not see. For these, as the second tale saies, folly towles the bell, and a number longs to heare it ring out, when the losse of Johns chicken is of more want then theirs; but, a rope out of it, it will one day be better. Ther are, as Hamlet saies, things cald whips in store.

The third jest of John shews morrally many things; amongst which, things, I meane workes, are so cobbled that, to rid it with quicknesse, John may beare it up and downe to the owner, while workmanship and time is merely abused — but it boots not to meddle in this, least some say, ne sutra, &c. But let me tel ye this, by the way, World: there are knaues in thy seames, that must be ript out. I, sayes the World; and such, I feare, was your father. O! no, sayes the critticke, he was the silly gentleman that staid while the foole brought home his boots, and so forfeited his bond, that his good conditions lay at gage for it. Marry, yes, saies the World; and was after canseld at the gallows: for such as her lies in wait to cosin simplycitie, and for a groat buy that which, well got, deserues a portague. At this the cinnick fretted: and heere they begin to challenge the combat; but a parly sounded, summoned them to the last tale with John to the cellar in the spittell; where, if they please, they may carouse freely, though they die deepe in scarlet, as many doe, till they loose themselues in the open streets. Such Diogenes sought at noone day with a lanthorne and a candell. Well, the World so buffeted the cinnicke at his owne weapon, that he playes with her, as weake fencers that carries flesh up and downe for others to dresse. Such was the cinnicke, onskilfull in guips and worldly flaunts, rather to play with short rods, and giue venies till all smarte againe; not in the braines, as the World did, but in the buttocks, as such doe, hauing their joses displaid, making them expert till they cry it up in the top of question.

Our sullen cinnicke sets by his glasse in malice, knits a betill brow till the roome grew darke againe, which the wanton World seeing, flings out of his cell, like a girle at barley brake, leauing the last couple in hell, away she gads, and neuer lookes behinde her. A whirlewinde, sayes the cinnicke, goe after!—is this all my thanks?—the old payment still!—will the World still reward mortality thus?—is vertue thus bedridden?—can she not helpe herselfe? and lookes up to heauen, as hee should say, some power assist! But there he sat, fretting in his owne grease, and, for ought I know, nobody came to help him.

CONCLUSIO.

Thus, gentlemen, as the kinde hostess salutes her guests, saying, You see your cheere, and you are welcome — so say I. It may bee you like it not. I am sorrier, you will say, these sallets were ill drest. Like enough; but good stomachs digest anything, and that it was a dry feast. The cinnicke bad [not] the World so much as drinck :—true, a worldling right, who, as the word is drinck before you goe, sets the cart before the horse, and sayes, goe before you drink, why may he not in his cell? — his betters will. J haue seene it in the gentlemens cellers—but I cry you mercy; there, I think, it is, drinck till you cannot goe. Bownce is the worlds motto there, till they discharge the braine of all good abearing, making the body breake the peace in euery corner: but blame me not, I am tedious; pardon my folly—writing of folly; if you knew, you would say hic mirum. Wherefore, if my pardon may be purchased, then so; if not, you may bid me keepe any fooles company.

FINIS.

NOTES.

Page 1, line 5. *Stultorum plena sunt omnia.*] Armin's motto reminds us of that assumed by La Societé de la Mère Folle de Dijon—*Numerus Stultorum infinitus est.* See Du Tilliot " Mémoires pour servir a l'Histoire de la Fête des Foux."—W. J. T.

Page 3, line 11. May beautifie our GLOBE in every line.] An allusion to the *Globe Theatre,* at which Armin was an actor.

Page 3, line 23. While they of Al-soules *gave ayme.*] " To giue aim" and " to cry aim" seem to have been synonymous of old, and were figurative phrases derived from archery, generally meaning *to consent to.* " To cry aim" occurs in " King John," act ii., sc. 1 (Collier's edit., vol. iv., p. 24), and elsewhere in Shakespeare. It may also be pointed out in the works of nearly all the popular writers of the same date. For a few instances, see Dodsley's Old Plays, last edit., vol. ii., p. 279.

Page 4, line 4. I goe in *motly.*] Motley was the term applied to the parti-coloured dress of jesters or clowns; such as that worn by Touchstone in " As you like it," the domestic fool in " All's well that ends well," &c.

Page 4, line 9. Not with your good *skene* head me.] A skene, or skean, was a species of knife or short sword used by the Irish; and called, in their language, *sgian* or *skian,* probably from the Icelandic *skeina,* to wound.

Page 5, line 7. She now begins to grow *bucksome* as a lightning before death.] The old meaning of " buxom" is *obedient.* In " Henry V.," act iii., sc. 6, Pistol talks of " buxom valour," meaning valour that was controllable, and under good command; but it does not seem very clear in what way Armin means to apply the word.

Page 5, line 19. No, nor to the Country, where seldom seene.] This and the five preceding lines are printed as prose in the original; perhaps for the purpose of saving room.

Page 5, line 23. One that was wise enough and *fond* enough.] The most common sense of " fond," of old, was foolish; and hence we may perhaps infer that our ancestors thought it *foolish* to be fond.

Page 5, line 20. And sold all for a glass prospective.] i. e. Such a glass as conjurors were in the habit of using.

Page 6, line 6. That is sharp *sauce* with bitter dyet.] For *sauce*, the original has *lance*, an obvious misprint.

Page 6, line 18. For as they (I) all for the most part.] *Ay* was almost invariably printed with a capital *I* at the period when this tract was published.

Page 7, line 23. Knowne to many, *loude* of any.] i. e. probably " *allow'd* of any," because he relied upon truth in his jests. It may, however, be a misprint for " loud *as* any."

Page 7, line 31. In motley cotes goes Jack Oates.] Jack Oates is a new name in the list of English Fools or Jesters, and obviously belongs to that class of the General Domestic Fool which the late Mr. Douce, in his Dissertation on the Clowns and Fools of Shakespeare, describes as being " silly by nature, yet cunning and sarcastical."—W. J. T.

Page 7, line 36. If it were possible such breathde hers to commaunde.] The meaning seems to be, that the World inquires, if it were possible that such persons as Jack Oates breathed hers to command, or at her command.

Page 8, line 8. Queene Richard, art come? quoth he.] " Queen Dick" is still an expression among the lower orders. How it came into use it is not, perhaps, possible to explain.

Page 9, line 18. At Christmas time, when great logs furnish the hall fire.]

> When icicles hang by the wall
> And Dick, the shepherd, blows his nail,
> And Tom bears logs into the hall. &c.
> " As you like it." Act v., sc. 2.

Page 9, line 22. A noyse of minstrels and a Lincolnshire bagpipe was provided.] A *noise* of minstrels meant of old a company of minstrels: thus, in Henry IV., Part 2, Act ii., sc. 4 (Collier's edit. iv., 379), we hear of " Sneak's noise," which the drawer was told to procure for the entertainment of Falstaff. In the first part of the same play, Shakespeare does not speak very favourably of " the drone of a Lincolnshire bagpipe;" but, from various authorities, it appears that it was an instrument then in much request. From what follows, in Armin, we learn the part of the family for which it was provided.

Page 13, line 29. They knockt to the dresser, and the dinner went up.]

The custom for the cook to knock on the dresser, when the dinner was ready to be placed upon table, is mentioned by many old writers. See Middleton's " Blurt Master Constable," Act ii., sc. 1; upon which the Rev. A. Dyce, in his edition of that dramatist's Works i., 247, makes the following note:—
" When dinner was ready, the cook used to knock on the dresser with his knife, as a signal for the servants to carry it into the hall." He adds a correction of an important error on the subject made by Reed and Nares.

Page 14, line 26. The knight and the rest all laught a good.] i. e. laughed *in good earnest*. The expression was common, and sufficient instances of its use may be seen in a note on Marlowe's " Rich Jew of Malta," in Dodsley's Old Plays, last edit. viii., p. 280. The words occur again on p. 21 and 32 of this tract.

Page 15, line 10. The knight perceiving the fooles *envie*.] i. e. the fool's *hatred:* " envy" was then constantly used with this meaning.

Page 15, line 25. They carde hence what their parents spin.] There is a play here upon the word *card*, as applied to the domestic operations of *carding and spinning* and gaming: " they card hence what their parents spin," means they wantonly disperse what their parents had industriously accumulated.

Page 16, line 3. The deuouring of *deuoutions* dyet.] We suspect some misprint here: possibly we ought to read " another's diet," the compositor having carried on the first part of the word " deuouring" to the next word but one.

Page 16, line 18. Two yards in compasse & a nayle I *reade*.] It may be doubtful whether we are to take " I read" literally, and that Armin had read this description of the uncouth dwarf, James Camber, in some work of the time; or whether we are to understand " I read" only in that sense in which our older authors sometimes employ *I rede*, i. e. I *advise* or *inform*. Probably, from what follows, the former was the case.

Page 16, line 22. But what that time Jemy a Camber was.] The custom of keeping a fool appears to have prevailed in the Scotch as generally as in any other of the European courts, and it may be presumed was retained for a long time among the nobility; since, among the curiosities shown at Glammis Castle, was, within these few years, the dress worn by the domestic fool belonging to the family. Among the Scotch wearers of Motley, the name of John Lowe, the king of Scotland's fool, holds a prominent place; while Archee and Muckle John figure among the professed jesters of the English court. The late Mr. Octavius Gilchrist published an interesting account of Archibald Armstrong, and his jests, in the *London Magazine* for Sept. 1824.—W. J. T.

Page 17, line 31 Who hearing the ordinance goe off, would aske what doe they now?] Jemmy Camber would ask; not the king, the last antecedent. Sufficient has been seen to show us that we must not be very critical, either as to Armin's grammar or style of composition.

Page 18, line 3. That of a maide had a *barne*.] A word still used in the north for a *child*.

Page 18, line 12. A sodaine *flaw* or gust rose.] This passage forms a brief but decisive explanation of the line in " Hamlet," Act v., sc.1.

" Should patch a wall to expel the winter's *flaw*,"

and other passages in Shakespeare, where the word " flaw" occurs. A "flaw" is a gust of wind. Boswell informs us that Dryden uses it generally for a storm, but such is not the case in the quotation he makes to support his position.

Page 18, line 35. For no way could I haue been a looser.] There is probably some misprint in the original copy in this sentence; for, as it stands, it is not intelligible.

Page 19, line 18. Wearing a loose kerchiefe, hanging downe backward.] This is curious, shewing that women of bad character at that time wore some peculiar kind of dress by which they were known. They are now recognised by other indications, quite as decisive.

Page 19, line 23. Giue me an Atchison.] " The meaning of the term ' Atchison,' as applied to coins," writes Mr. Laing, of Edinburgh, " is thus explained. Thomas Atcheson was assay-master of the Mint at Edinburgh during the minority of James VI., and also during the reign of Mary. His name was given in derision to base metal coins which then were in circulation, and which, as Bishop Nicolson mentions (Scottish Hist. Library, p. 326, 8vo edit.), were in the year 1587 ' cryed down by Proclamation, because counterfeit in England and other foreign parts.' Nicolson, however, at p. 34, confounds this Atcheson with an Englishman, who wrote a treatise on the Gold Mines in Scotland, which was printed some years ago for the Bannatyne Club; and Gough, correcting the Bishop's error, only commits a greater mistake."

Page 20, line 25. He did so, but the glove lay still.] In running at the glove, it was placed upon the ground, and the art was for a horseman, at speed, to take it up on the point of his lance. Running at the ring was different, for there the object to be carried away was suspended. Explanations may be found in Strutt's " Sports and Pastimes."

Page 21, line 26. Jemy, who was, as you haue heard, a *tall* low man.] This reads like a contradiction in terms; but " tall," in the time of our author,

NOTES. 61

did not usually mean lofty of stature, but *courageous* and *bold*. Shakespeare so uses it with reference to Sir Andrew Aguecheek in " Twelfth Night," act i., sc. 3 (Collier's edit. iii. 330), " He's as *tall* a man as any's in Illyria." Instances of the same kind in other authors of the time are innumerable.

Page 22, line 14. The Earle of Morton's castle at *da Keth*.] No doubt misprinted for *Dalkeith*.

Page 25, line 8. Jemy rose, made him ready.] To make *ready* meant of old merely to *dress*, and to be ready was to be dressed. It was the commonest form of expression.

Page 25, line 25. He that *gard* all men till jeare.] i. e. He that made all men to jest. Mr. Holloway, in his Gen. Dict. of Provincialisms, derives the verb to *gar*, i. e. to compel or make, from the Danish *gior*. Spenser employs it in his " Shepherd's Calendar" for April :—

"Tell me, good Hobbinol, what *gars* thee greet ;"

and it is still in use in the north of England as well as in Scotland.

Page 25, line 34. Through the sense of sinne.] Perhaps we ought to read, " through the seas of sin." It seems an error of the press in the original.

Page 27, line 27. When 'a peard most holy.] i. e. When *he appear'd* most holy. Shakespeare repeatedly makes his characters in familiar dialogue use " 'a" for *he*. Few of his contemporaries adopt this practice so frequently.

Page 28, line 17. But thus with *supposes* he plays alone.] Shakespeare uses the word " supposes" for suppositions in " The Taming of the Shrew," and in " Titus Andronicus." Gascoyne had done so before him throughout his translation of the *Suppositi* of Ariosto.

Page 28, line 25. Such a hurly-burly in the roome, that passes.] i. e. that passes, or *surpasses*, belief. The expression was common.

Page 28, line 3. Found all this levell coyle.] Perhaps we ought to read, " found all this *lewd* or *wicked* coil or confusion."

Page 29, line 29. In the country, quoth hee, where God is a good man.] This expression is put into Dogberry's mouth in " Much Ado About Nothing," act iii., sc 5; and it is also found in the interlude of " Lusty Juventus," in the " Merry Jest of Robin Hood," and in Burton's " Anatomy of Melancholy."

Page 30, line 7. And got the foole's head under his arme and bob'd his nose.] The plough-jogger was an early adept in boxing, and got Leonard's head, as we now express it, " in Chancery." The expression is the more applicable since the appointment of *Vice*-chauncellors, so called, perhaps, from the tenacity with which they hold suitors who are unlucky enough to get into any of their courts.

NOTES.

Page 30, line 35. Who, *soothing* up his humours.] The original, by a misprint, has "who *something* up his humours."

Page 31, line 19. Then to *vere* at his losses sodainely.] There is probably an error in the press in this passage: perhaps we might read "than to *vexe* at his losses suddenly."

Page 32, line 13. Aloud he cries Dmee! Dmee! Dmee!] Most likely an abbreviation of "Dear me"!

Page 36, line 21. His song of *Dirries* Farie] Part of this song is given afterwards. See p. 38.

Page 36, line 23. Like the poter of the ale-fat.] i. e. like the poker of the ale-vat, in consequence of the "barm" or yeast upon his face to take out the fire.

Page 37, line 24. In the towne of Esam.] i. e. Evesham.

Page 37, line 36, They went to Partiar.] i. e. Pershore.

Page 38, line 6. They of the towne, loth to lose his company *desirued* to haue it so.] *Sic* in the old copy, but probably we ought to read *desired* for "desirued."

Page 38, line 13. My hart aked, &c.] This shews that Armin, the author, was one of the players on this occasion, and perhaps the performer of the clown's parts in the company.

Page 38, line 24. To weepe in kindnesse, and laugh in extremes.] "Extremes" is here used in the sense in which Shakespeare not unfrequently employs it. See "Winters Tale," act iv., sc. 3; "Troilus and Cressida," act iv., sc. 2; "Romeo and Juliet," act iv., sc. 1., &c.

Page 38, line 34. Mistris Annis, M. Thomas, under a tree mending of shoone.] The joke seems to be that the fool, at the commencement of each line, inserted some of the names of the parties before whom he was singing: the song by itself ran thus:—

> "*As I went to Derries Faire*
> *There was I ware of a jolly begger,*
> *Under a tree mending of shoone,*
> *Night-braue beggars euery one.*"

According to the license in the rhyming of old ballads, "begger," or "beggare," as it would be spelt, would be sufficient rhyme for "Faire." We have no other trace of this song; but as Armin does not insert it, and adds, "And so forward," we may presume that it was well known.

Page 39, line 5. Buy any FLAWRE.] Sic in orig., but perhaps a misprint for some word beginning with the letters p, in the pronunciation of which Jack Miller was "plagued." Possibly we ought to read *prawnes*.

Page 39, line 10. And euer as he hit the on word.] It may be doubted whether we ought to read "the *one* word," or to suppose "*on* the" transposed in the printing.

Page 40, line 3. There was no little boot to bid ront.] Some misprint has obscured the sense here. Ought we to read "There was no little boot to be rid on't?"

Page 40, line 31. That Bankes, his horse, with all his strength cannot draw them out.] One of the innumerable allusions to a person of the name of Bankes, who had trained a small horse to perform many wonderful feats. There is hardly a comic writer between 1590 and 1620 who does not introduce some notice of Bankes and his horse Marocco. A supposed dialogue between them, called *Maroccus Extaticus,* was printed in 1595, from which we learn the important fact that the horse was bay. After exhibiting him throughout this kingdom, Bankes took his horse abroad, where it seems to have been suspected that the animal was a fiend in disguise, and Bankes a conjuror. We learn the fate of both in the mock-romance of "Don Zara del Fogo," not printed until 1656, but written much earlier. "Finally," (says the unknown author), having of a long time proved himselfe the ornament of the British clime, travailing to Rome with his master, they were both burned by commandment of the pope." Marginal note to page 114. Bankes's horse is immortalised by Shakespeare in "Love's Labour's Lost," act i., sc. 2.

Page 41, line 9. Forsooth Wil. Sommers.] This well-known Jester of Henry VIII. is made, as it were, the hero of T. Nash's "Summers Last Will and Testament," a comic shew, written about 1593, and printed in 1600. An accurate reprint of it is given in "Dodsley's Old Plays," last edit., vol. ix. "A pleasant History of the Life and Death of Will Summers" was printed early, but no edition of it now seems to be known, but one in 1676, which was reprinted in 1794, with a portrait of Summers looking through a casement. We copy the following jest relating to him from Samuel Rowland's tract, called "Good and Bad Newes," 1622, 4to.

"Will Sommers once unto King Harry came,
And in a serious shew himselfe did frame
To goe to London, taking of his leaue.
Stay, William (quoth the king) I doe perceiue
You are in haste; but tell me your occasion:
Let me prevail thus by a friends perswasion.—
Quoth he, if thou wilt know, Ile tell thee marry:
I goe to London for Court-newes, old Harry.—
Goest thither from the Court to hear Court-newes?
This is a tricke, Sommers, that makes me muse.

Oh, yes (quoth William) citizens can show
Whats done in Court ere thou and I doe know.
If an Embassador be comming over,
Before he doe arrive and land at Dover
They know his master's message and intent,
Ere thou canst tell the cause why he is sent.
If of a Parliament they doe but heare,
They know what lawes shall be enacted there.
And, therefore, for a while, adue Whitehall.
Harry, Ile bring thee newes home, lyes and all."

We quote the above from the original very rare volume in the library of the Rt. Hon. Lord Francis Egerton, M.P.; but a very excellent reprint of it has been recently made by Edward V. Utterson, Esq., consisting, however, of only sixteen copies. Thus, each of these is scarcely less a prize than the original. We may add that Will Sommers figures conspicuously in S. Rowley's " When you see me you know me," a historical play, on the events of the reign of Henry VIII., printed in 1605.

Page 41, line 20. Leane he was, hollow-eyde, as all report.] This description of Will Sommers's person accords very well with the rare print of him by Delaram, described by Granger in his " Biographical History of England" (i. p. 116, ed. 1779), and also with the portrait of him in the frontispiece to the first volume of Sir Henry Ellis's " Original Letters illustrative of English History," which is taken from Henry the Eight's Psalter, preserved among the Royal MSS. in the British Museum. It does not, however, by any means correspond with the admirable picture by Holbein of a merry knave looking through a leaded casement, described in the Guide to the Pictures at Hampton Court, as one of Henry the Eight's jesters, but traditionally said to be a portrait of Will Sommers. A fine copy of this portrait, we understand, is preserved at Audley End, the seat of the Right Honourable Lord Braybrooke.—W. J. T.

Page 42, line 8. Will Sommers, in no little credit at the King's Court.] Our author speaks this with truth, since, notwithstanding Henry's well-known fondness for these motley followers, Will is almost the only one of them whose memory has survived. Patch and Sexton are named in Henry's Household Book; and Mr. Douce, who supposes Patch to be only another name for Fool, states that he was given to Henry by Wolsey. Will Sommers, in all probability, owes his reputation rather to the uniform kindness with which he used his influence over bluff Harry, than to his wit or folly ; and one of the latest instances of this conduct is so honourable to the poor

NOTES. 65

jester, that it is only justice to his memory to repeat it as told by Granger:—

Will Sommers was sometimes a servant in the family of Richard Faimor, Esq., of Eston Weston, in Northamptonshire, ancestor to the Earl of Pomfret. This gentleman was found guilty of a *præmunire* in the reign of Henry VIII., for sending eightpence and a couple of shirts to a priest convicted of denying the king's supremacy, who was then a prisoner in the goal at Buckingham. The rapacious monarch seized whatever he was possessed of, and reduced him to a state of miserable dependence. Will Sommers, touched with compassion for his unhappy master, is said to have dropped some expressions, in the king's last illness, which reached the conscience of the merciless prince, and to have caused the remains of his estate, which had been dismembered, to be restored to him.—W. J. T.

Page 43, line 34. By my *vusse*.] So in the original, but the meaning of the asseveration it is not easy to comprehend: possibly " By my *vows*."

Page 45, line 1. And are for mirth inserted into stage-playes.] Referring to such dramatic pieces as " When you see me you know me," by Rowley, before-mentioned.

Page 45, line 3. There are some will affirme it now living at Greenwich.] We have no account of the precise period of the death of Will Sommers, but it might not have happened more than fifty or sixty years before Armin wrote; and people who recollected Sommers and his pranks might still be living in Greenwich and elsewhere.

Page 46, line 9. That remarkable work of his tombe.] P. Martyr, in his *Comment in lib. Samuelis* (2nd Samuel, cap. 18) relates a remarkable anecdote, which may here be very properly introduced. It appears that the Cardinal was in the habit of frequently visiting his tomb at Windsor to watch the progress of the work. On one of these occasions he was accompanied by his fool, or jester, who, seeing him enter the monument, said, You do well to go into your tomb during your lifetime, for you will never enter it when dead.

This was probably the same fool who, congratulating the Cardinal upon receiving that dignity, expressed a wish that he might soon see him Pope. Why so? inquired the Cardinal. Marry replied he, St. Peter, who was a fisherman, instituted fasts that fish might fetch a better price, and, since your eminence was bred a butcher, you would, no doubt, order us to eat meat, instead of fish, for the sake of your trade.

The readers of " Cavendish's Life of Woolsey" will remember the Cardinal's requesting Norris to present the King with this poor fool, and the almost pathetic manner in which he describes the fool's unwillingness to be separated from his old master.—W. J. T.

F

NOTES.

Page 47, line 9. Had hee not poysoned himselfe.] The notion, founded upon a passage in Cavendish's "Life of Wolsey," that the Cardinal poisoned himself, has been controverted with success, by Pegge. See Gentlemen's Magazine, vol. xxv., p. 25.

Page 48, line 16. O weel to make them great, make ourselves.] There is probably an error of the press in this passage, which renders the sense obscure. The whole paragraph is not very intelligible.

Page 49, line 22. *Lesse* such as let him not alone.] i. e., "*Unless* such," &c.

Page 49, line 23. As *a* liude, so *a* dyde.] *i. e.* As *he* liv'd so *he* died. See p. 27, and the note: this is another instance of the same kind.

Page 49, line 27. But neither John a nods, nor *John a dreames.*] "John a-dreams" is mentioned in Hamlet.

" A dull and muddy-mettled rascal, peak,
Like John a-dreams, unpregnant of my cause."

The commentators introduce notes about Jack-a-Lent, Jack-a-Lanthern, and John-a-Droynes; but they were unacquainted with this passage in Armin's tract about "John a nods and John a dreames," both names, perhaps, meant for the same person.

Page 49, line 29. Like your tobacco to *tast* strong.] The original by an obvious misprint has "to *fast* strong."

Page 50, line 1. Snapping his fingers barber-like.] The snapping, or, as it is sometimes spelt, knacking, of their fingers by barbers is noticed by many old writers. "Amongst the rest let not the barber be forgotten; and look that he be an excellent fellow, and one that can *snap his fingers* with dexterity." "Greenes *Tu Quoque*" in Dodsley's Old Plays, last edit., vol. vii., p. 31. See also Ben Jonson's "Epicœne," act i., sc. 2. Lily, in his "Midas," 1592, introduces a barber, who says to his apprentice, "Thou knowest, boy, I haue taught thee the *knacking of the hands.*"

Page 50, line 21. To meet with B. Nowell.] Dean Nowell of course all are acquainted with, but it is questionable why Armin places a capital B. before his name, as he never was a bishop, and his Christian name was Alexander. Afterwards Armin calls him " B. Deane."

Page 50, line 23. He gaue *them* a groat.] We ought to read *him* for " them."

Page 54, line 18. As his picture in Christ's Hospital (now to be seene) can witnesse.] This picture of a domestic fool was in existence some years ago, but nobody was able to state whom it represented. Armin's tract will

NOTES.

enable those who, we presume, now have charge of the portrait to decide the question.

Page 55, line 8. There are, as Hamlet saies, things cald whips in store.] No such passage is to be found in Shakespeare's Hamlet, as it has come down to us, either in the editions of 1603, 1604, or in any later impression. Possibly Armin may refer to the old Hamlet which preceded Shakespeare's tragedy; but this seems unlikely, as he was an actor in the same theatre as that for which Shakespeare wrote.

Page 55, line 14. Least some say *ne sutra.*] Of course a misprint for *ne sutor.* Armin did not add the rest of the proverb, because it was so well known.

Page 55, line 22. Which, well got, deserues a *portague.*] Probably a Portuguese gold coin.

Page 55, line 33.] And giue *Venies* till all smarte againe.] *Venie,* or, as it is sometimes spelt, *Venu* or *Venny,* was a very common fencing term, meaning the onset, from the French *Venir.* See " Loves Labours Lost," vol. ii., p. 347, Collier's Shakespeare, where the word, as in most instances of its use, is figuratively employed.

Page 56, line 3. Like a girle at barley brake, leauing the last couple in hell.] Barrley-break seems to have been a game much resembling what is now called Prisoner's Base, or Prisoner's Bars. " Leaving the last couple in hell" was a phrase in it, and the allusions to it, in old writers, are endless.

LONDON :
F. SHOBERL, JUN., 51, RUPERT STREET, HAYMARKET,
PRINTER TO H. R. H. PRINCE ALBERT.

Printed in Great Britain by
Amazon.co.uk, Ltd.,
Marston Gate.